Tony Cointreau

A
Gift
of
Love

Lessons Learned From My Work and
Friendship with Mother Teresa

Tony Cointreau

PROSPECTA PRESS

Westport and New York

Published by
Prospecta Press
An imprint of Easton Studio Press
P.O. Box 3131
Westport, CT 06880
(203) 571-0781

www.prospectapress.com

Manufactured in the United States of America

FIRST EDITION

Cover and book design by Barbara Aronica-Buck for Booktrix
Photograph of the author by Stephen Mosher

Hardcover ISBN: 978-1-63226-049-9
eBook ISBN: 978-1-63226-050-5

For all those I have loved,
Till we meet again

"When we are born, we cry,
and the world rejoices.
When we die, we rejoice,
and the world cries."

An ancient Buddhist saying

Contents

Foreword

In 2002, after twelve years of volunteering in Mother Teresa's homes, I was sitting on the porch of my country home in Vermont, looking out on six magnificent mountain ranges, and listening to the many hours of tapes I had recorded every day after work. It was then that I knew that the best way I could now be of service was to share with others whatever I, as a layperson, had learned—not only through my years of service with Mother Teresa, but also through the way I had handled caregiving and the deaths of those I loved in my own family.

After Mother Teresa's death, I would sit in front of the computer and silently ask her to help me to write about caring for loved ones. I could immediately feel her presence over my right shoulder, and it felt as if I entered another dimension for the next several hours. When I "awoke," I was astonished to read what I had written. It was then that I knew how much help I had been given from a higher source.

Mother Teresa had responded to me from the first day we met, because I always treated her as a human being. Most people, even her own nuns, treated her as a living saint, but she was so humble that such adulation made her uncomfortable. She used to sit and talk with me for long periods of time, "about everything and nothing."

Back in Calcutta, whenever Mother Teresa had asked me to sing for her on her little terrace, I never said "No." And when I asked her to help me write, she also never said "No." What a blessing—thank you, Mother!

In 1979, when I saw a magazine photograph of one of Mother Teresa's volunteers carrying a dying man in his arms, I knew in an instant that I had to become a part of this work. It was certainly not a religious calling, but a simple calling to give something of myself to others. I felt that if I could comfort one dying person, my life would have had purpose.

It took me ten years to enter the world that I had only seen a glimpse of in that magazine article. When I did, it was during the worst of the AIDS crisis in the United States, in a hospice called "Gift of Love" in New York City, which had been opened by Mother Teresa in 1985. It had room for fifteen dying men, most of them from a world I had never known—a world of drugs, poverty, and crime, a far cry from the privileged life of châteaus in Europe that I had been brought up in, and later on, the world of show business in which I had been able to fulfill some of my greatest dreams.

In the years to come, these men, who were dying of AIDS and had never been given much of a chance in life, taught me not only about the many ways to help others die in an atmosphere of peace and love, but also how to enjoy the richness of living our lives fully until the very end.

It made no difference whether I was in Calcutta or New York, the lessons I learned were the same. Even the language was no barrier in India. We communicated in a language all its own—a language of unconditional love, and what we gave to each other was truly a gift of love.

CHAPTER 1

A Time to Be Born, A Time to Die

"Goodbye, my darling."

The evening dusk was falling outside the hospital window as I sat on the edge of my beloved Aunt Tata's bed and prattled on about the inconsequential happenings of my day. After years of caring for her through devastating illnesses, I was not able to acknowledge the fact that she was in the last hours of her life. Finally she looked into my eyes, and in little more than a whisper, said, "Goodbye, my darling."

I quickly kissed her and got up to leave, for fear that I might tire her if I stayed. That night she passed on with only an intern at her side.

It was at the cemetery, when I first saw the coffin, that I understood that someone I had loved all my life was in that box and would never come back. At that moment I was forced to summon all the self-control that had been drummed into me from an early age—a discipline dictated by phrases such as "Men don't cry" and "Bluebloods never give in!"

Now it was over, and I had missed a precious opportunity—the last chance to express my affection and appreciation for a life that had so enriched my own.

In my heart I knew she would gladly have allowed

me to share in one of the two great transformations of
life—her death. But in those last days I had been too
frightened to face the overwhelming emotions that I
had been taught to sublimate since childhood.

Later on I remembered that that last evening had
been the only time she had ever said "Goodbye" to me.
Until then she had always left me with the words "*Au
revoir*"—"Till we meet again." By saying "Goodbye" for
the first time, she showed me that she understood the
agony I could not face and loved me enough to send a
gentle message that took me years to comprehend. She
knew me so well that she had no doubt that I would
someday learn to accept my emotions and face the
deaths around me with a courage born of unconditional
love—the same courage and unconditional love that she
had shown me all my life.

This was not a quick transformation or an easy lesson to learn. Each time I ran away from the inevitable
when it was happening to those I loved most in the
world, I vowed, "Next time I'll get it right!"

My father, Jacques, was born into a prominent but small
French family that had created an international success
with Cointreau Liqueurs in the late-nineteenth century.
By the time he came along in 1901, their modest origins
had been forgotten, and although they had a habit
of pinching pennies, they fully enjoyed a privileged
lifestyle.

My mother, Dorothee, on the other hand, came
from an aristocratic Boston family whose fortune was

long gone when she was born in 1900 (she went to her grave without my father's knowing that she was one year older than he). Her family's aim in life was to keep up appearances while making do with what little they had.

My parents, who were approaching their forties when they married, were very much in love and well suited to each other. They lived in their own affluent cocoon and shied away from the harsh realities of life that might threaten the emotional armor that they had built up around themselves.

Slowly, over the years, I learned to follow my parents' example and did my best to close down my own emotions, attempting to hide the feelings that lay just under the surface of my too-sensitive skin.

I was thirty-eight years old when I first read about *Nirmal Hriday,* Mother Teresa's home for destitute men and women who were picked up from the gutters and slums of Calcutta and taken to a place where the worms were carefully removed from their bodies; where they were washed, clothed, fed and put in a comfortable bed with clean sheets. But most of all they had someone to hold their hand and love them before they went home to whatever God they believed in.

One man asked the little nun, "Why are you doing this?"

Mother Teresa's answer was characteristically simple. She replied, "Because I love you."

His last words on earth were, "I've lived my life like an animal, and now I'm going to die like a king."

I did not need to read any further. My heart had

already begun to race. In an instant, I knew that the dormant possibilities for the more meaningful life I had been seeking could become a reality. Somehow I had to find a way to follow this road wherever it might lead.

Ten years and what seemed like a lifetime later, I took the plunge and made my first pilgrimage to where I felt my destiny was leading me. I didn't know why, but I had no doubt that I had a "calling" to share in this work with the dying.

I was forty-eight years old when I arrived in India in November of 1989, saying, "My dream has finally become a reality." However, it did not take more than a few hours in Calcutta for me to realize that I was totally unprepared for its unrelenting poverty. For four days I was forced to remain there, waiting for an available flight home and trying to deal with the emotional crisis that Calcutta had precipitated. I did not realize the importance of it at the time, but this experience in Calcutta miraculously opened the floodgates of my pent-up emotions, and permitted me to cry for the first time in my adult life.

Upon my return to the United States, my partner Jim Russo and I immediately went to visit his sister, Louise, who had become like a sister to me as well. She was in a hospital in Vermont, dying of cancer at the age of fifty-nine. Now, unlike other times in my life when loved ones were dying, I was able to stay with Louise until the end, holding her hand and telling her how much she was loved.

A few months after Louise's death, I picked up the phone and called a hospice in Greenwich Village in New York City—a home that had been opened by the little nun who had inspired me from the beginning—and asked if they could use a volunteer. The home was for destitute men dying of AIDS, a disease that in 1990 was a death sentence. At that time the medical community did not know how it was transmitted or have any effective way to treat it. Fear and ignorance were rampant, and even my own doctor advised me not to go there—it was too dangerous.

I told him, "If we can't do this for other human beings, then there is no hope."

On April 4, 1990, I began to volunteer at the hospice called "Gift of Love," which had been opened on December 24, 1985, by Mother Teresa as a birthday gift to Jesus. Because of the enormous stigma of AIDS, most of the patients had been abandoned not only by society but also by their families. As Sister Maria Lucy, the nun in charge of the home, said to me when I first went for an interview, "Tony, *we* are their families!"

These dying men, who had never been given much of a chance in life, taught me during the next twelve years not only about the many ways to help others die in an atmosphere of peace and love, but also how to enjoy the richness of living our lives fully until the very end.

It seems that our society considers what should be the normal transition of death to be a taboo subject. We tend to pretend that it does not exist. But in denying the reality of what is happening, we not only rob the dying person of any feeling of comfort, we also insist on creating a make-believe world where nothing ever changes. The truth is that all life is change—constant change. Without that, life would be stagnant and not really worthwhile.

What we often think of as the most complicated of situations is really very simple. With a little common sense and a lot of love, facing the fearful situation we call death can be transformed into one of the greatest of gifts for ourselves and our loved ones.

Of course, in no way would anyone imply that there is no emotional pain involved for the caregiver. The pain of a loss can be excruciating, but it need never defeat you. It can tear you apart, but you can rise again, and if given the opportunity to aid and participate in the final days, hours, and moments of someone's life, *you*, the participant, will never be the same either. Any love and comfort that we give leaves both the giver and the receiver in a different realm than before.

There are many taboos born of our fear of the unknown. However, with some basic information to start with, and the opportunity to break out of the mold for even a few moments, we can open the door to a new understanding of others and to the reason we are put on this earth in the first place.

My not having been able to face the reality of death and dying throughout my early life is not unusual in our society. But during my twelve years volunteering in Mother Teresa's homes for the dying, I learned the invaluable power that exists in:

- Listening
- Touching
- Choices
- Humor
- Taking nothing for granted
- Non-judgment
- Respect
- Music
- Unconditional love
- Faith

The importance of all these and more became clear to me as I tended to each unique human being in my care.

Because the patients at Gift of Love were given the freedom to express their thoughts on the process of dying as it was happening, no one was forced to feel alone—ever—thereby lessening the fear of the unknown and even sometimes the physical pain. If the mind is at peace, the physical body will not feel the same agony as it would if it were rigid with fear.

In my years of working with the dying, I—who had been so filled with terror at the thought of human mortality—helped more than one hundred men during their final months, days, and hours. This book is a distillation of some of the things I learned that helped them. And I discovered that every day is a miracle and that the journey never ends.

CHAPTER 2

Listening

"And all I did was listen."

One of the first things Mother Teresa ever told me was, "Tony, if you'll just listen, you'll find that there is something beautiful about each of these men." And, before long, I could see it.

I loved them all.

And I lost them all.

But through the years I learnt my lessons as I went along—both by watching the nuns and other volunteers and by following my own instincts. Each situation (and there were dozens every day) was as different and unique as the men were.

At first all I tried to do was gain the men's trust by showing them that I was sincere about my work. This meant mopping floors, washing stairs on my hands and knees, cooking (not my greatest talent), answering the phone or the door, changing diapers on grown men, taking our patients to the clinics and waiting for hours in emergency rooms for doctors who were helpless to do much, if anything, for people with AIDS. In essence, it meant proving to one and all that I was happy to do the most menial of tasks with a smile and a willingness at any time to drop my work and just listen to a young man who was anxious to unburden himself to a friend.

From the beginning the Sisters had explained that although my duties would be whatever came up at any given moment, the most important work of all would be to listen to the patients—not only to what they said but also to the things that some of them sometimes found difficult to articulate.

A young man called Robert, who (I was told by another volunteer) had been in a prison "with the really bad boys," was having a difficult time keeping up the "tough guy" image he felt he had to portray.

Although Robert hated to show his vulnerability, I suspected that he had been conditioned (not unlike myself) never to give in to any show of weakness in front of others. He did, however, often like to complain, so I just listened to the good and the bad. I knew I had made some headway the day he confided to me, "I hope I pass the summer, and if I pass the summer, then I can go in peace."

Later that afternoon, as I was leaving, he leaned over the banister and called down, "Tony!"

I looked up and said, "Yes, Robert."

For a moment he seemed at a loss for words, and then stammered, "Your collar's crooked."

The words Robert used were immaterial—I knew instinctively that that was the only way Robert was able to express, "Thanks for being here and listening."

I once tried to make a list of the things we respond to from the day we are born, and one of the first ways we bond with a parental figure is by communicating our feelings through tears or laughter. Mother and father then have to listen carefully to how we make ourselves understood so they can react accordingly. A loving parent usually ends up able to interpret each nuance in their child's sounds and demeanor.

Later, when we learn to express ourselves with words, we have a deep need to share each new experience with someone who cares. It may be a parent, a schoolteacher, a grandparent, a friend, or all of the above. But one person's close attention to our joys, our sorrows and our endless questions are a vital part of our growth—especially while every little happening in our lives is still the most exciting thing in the world to us.

As we reach adolescence, it becomes even more confusing if there is no one there for us to relate our concerns to about the emotional and physical changes taking place. How many troubled teenagers say that all they really miss is a parent or mentor to spend time with—someone who will take the time to listen.

Loneliness and fear take root early on in our lives when we feel we have no one to talk to. And in the twenty-first century, when both parents often have full-time careers, it becomes increasingly difficult for a mother and father to find the time to listen to what is happening in their children's lives. Emotional issues are usually the first to be put on the back burner and are considered "normal" for that age. Because parents often don't have the time to spare, they forget the immediacy of the trials of their own youth. They figure these are minor problems that can be dealt with at a later time—

a time that sometimes doesn't come before enormous damage has already been done.

In my grandparents' day, before the world was filled with high technology, families lived in a home where the children were usually born and where there was always a place for the older generation to live out their lives. The cycle of birth and death was not a mystery to young people who were active participants in all aspects of family life.

Today women cannot be faulted for choosing the safer option of a hospital birth for their child. Neither can they be faulted for no longer being able to care for an elderly family member in their home. But the sad part of all this is that it has helped create a new world where children are not taught the natural progressions of life. Now the aging process of a beloved grandparent is often, at best, kept at a distance while a staff of strangers takes care of them in what is now called "assisted living." In these facilities all responsibility is taken off the family's shoulders as the necessary level of care is upgraded with time.

This situation enables the next generation to ignore the final stages of life that the older person goes through and does not give the younger ones the benefit of the wisdom, love, or connection to those responsible for their heritage. And so the charade continues, while we permit ourselves to hide our heads in the sand and pretend that the impersonal care and feeding of those who raised us are adequate substitutes for our love.

The tragedy of abandonment of the ones who have

nurtured us, who desperately need our love at the end of their lives, was overwhelmingly shown to me when I went to an assisted living home in New York City called Atria, where my old nurse Lucy, who had cared for my brother and me when we were born, was living.

When I arrived, I was told that Lucy was at a doctor's appointment with her aide, so I went into a comfortable little sitting room to wait for them to come home.

When I sat down, I noticed an elderly lady in a wheelchair talking on the phone with her son, pleading with him to come visit her. I could tell she was speaking in the most diplomatic way possible, so as not to anger him.

At the end of their conversation, I nearly fell out of my chair when I heard her say, in the sweetest possible way, "But, darling, you only live a block away."

In no way am I condemning anyone for the way their lives are dictated in this new age we live in. But it is no excuse not to wake up and make your presence known to the millions of elderly or dying people waiting in vain day after day for the sound of a familiar voice.

My great-grandmother, Louisa Cointreau, was a remarkable woman who had been decorated by the French government for her work creating hospitals and taking care of wounded soldiers during World War I. By the time I met her in 1947, when I was six years old, at her château in the Loire Valley where my parents and my brother and I spent most of our summers, she was senile and remembered nothing from one moment to the next.

Nevertheless, she lived at home under the care of her family and participated in all their activities.

In spite of her senility she remembered everything that had happened years before, and spent hours with me poring over old photograph albums and telling me who each person was. I only wish we had had more time together and that I had known her before she became senile. Today I realize that my having listened to her relate her history was something that gave her great joy, and, for my part, something I will always treasure. Of course, she never had any idea who my brother and I were, and every few minutes would ask anyone passing by, "Who are those two little American boys?"

Not only was it no bother to tell her periodically that we were her great-grandchildren, but it always pleased me that the thought of our being related made her so happy.

Grandmère Louisa, as I called her, died peacefully in her own bed at home in 1952, with her family and friends at her side.

But I have found that even when human beings have been forced to spend their whole lives in a state of lonely desperation, at the end, the door to their emotions is always ready to be opened. Although it may be only days or even hours before death that they find that loving ear, the deafening quiet of a lifetime can be erased forever in those last moments. It is never too late to make the connection, especially when it is a connection born of love.

From my first day at Gift of Love I found the men

anxious to share their varied and often tragic stories with me, and as the years went by, I thought that nothing could shock or surprise me anymore. But every time I started to feel that I had heard or seen it all, someone would come along and knock me off my pedestal of complacency and teach me one more lesson about the complexity of the human condition and the importance of honoring each of my friends' unique stories.

One of these men was Abraham, one of the sweetest human beings who ever walked into Gift of Love. He soon managed to open my eyes to a possibility in the range of suffering that I had not yet contemplated.

Abraham had come to us in the last stages of AIDS, with a prognosis of days or a few weeks at most to live. The doctors had been preparing for an operation to attempt to save his sight, but now they told us that it was too late to even try. Shortly after he received the news, one of the Sisters asked me to go up to his room and talk with him.

The moment I walked into his room, he brought me up to date on the discouraging prognosis. When I asked him how he felt about it, he said, "I'm at peace. I'm not afraid of dying but I don't want to suffer." I told him that the greatest fear we all had was of suffering.

Then I noticed that the beautiful long black hair that I had seen before had now been cut short. As soon as I mentioned that he had cut his hair, his peaceful demeanor began to crumble and he started to cry.

"Oh, Tony, you don't know. You just don't know. Please don't tell anyone—nobody knows—but when I

became sick I was in the last stages of gender reassign-
ment. My dream was to become a woman. Now that
dream can never be. It's too late. I've become too sick
and know I won't even be able to *die* the way I wanted—
as a woman."

Every day after that I went into his room and every
day he always had the sweetest smile on his face. Sometimes we would just sit silently together. Words were no
longer necessary. We had created a bond of love and
understanding.

And the only thing that had made him cry was when
he knew that he would not die as a woman. What I
believe helped make it bearable was that he could safely
share it with another human being who would never
judge him.

I always considered it a gift when a terminally ill man felt
comfortable enough to open his heart and his life to me,
a virtual stranger, and allow me to share in the preparation for his final journey. What I didn't realize at first was
that in confiding their deepest human secrets they were
releasing many layers of confusion and hurt, which then
allowed them to find a peace that had eluded them for
a lifetime.

None of us has to be a genius to make a difference
in someone's life or death. It takes no great intellect or
training. It's only a question of sincere listening and gen-
uine caring. This can be the final gift from the person
who knows you best in the world, or from a total
stranger.

One afternoon I was alone doing some boring task in the kitchen (peeling potatoes seemed to be one of my specialties) when a new patient named Joe came downstairs to the kitchen door and asked, "Can I talk to you?"

I said, "Sure, Joe. Just let me take off my apron and we can sit in the little office by the front door."

When my earthly eyes looked at Joe I saw a sickly, long-time drug addict with most of his teeth missing. It would have been hard for me to guess his age.

He took a seat and said, "Tony, the doctor told me that besides having AIDS, my body is filled with cancer and I don't have long to live.

"I've been a drug addict since the age of fifteen. Now I'm thirty-seven going on ninety-seven, and I'm probably going to die soon. All the friends I ever had are dead from drugs or AIDS. There's no one left."

He went on to say, "I loved my mother very much, but I'm glad she's dead too and did not have to live to see me in this condition.

"Although I was brought up and lived my whole life on the lower East side of Manhattan in some of the scariest parts of the city—places you would never want to bring up a child—I'm grateful that God has been good to me and has allowed me to survive longer than anybody I knew.

"Believe me, everything that has happened to me, I brought upon myself. I've spent a good part of my life in jail but I'm still in there pitching. I'm not giving up."

I listened quietly while Joe recounted the hardships of his life, the years of addiction, the years in jail, the pain of losing everyone around him, and even the feeling of uselessness of his life.

After Joe finished relating his story, he seemed almost lighthearted. Somehow he looked younger to me, as though a burden had been lifted from his frail shoulders.

Before getting up to go back upstairs, he held onto my hand and said, "Thank you. Thank you. I love you, man. I don't know you but I love you, man. I know you've got it right *here*."

And he put his hand on his heart.

And all I did was listen.

CHAPTER 3

Touch

"Sometimes it's the only medicine."

The first time I was aware of the healing power behind the simple act of touching a person in a loving way was when my mother and I arrived at the hospital after the doctors had amputated my aunt Tata's leg below the knee. We had decided to wait at home (only a few blocks away) during the operation and came back minutes after she had been wheeled back into her room.

My aunt had been stoic throughout the pain of gangrene, which had been caused by a hospital error when they blocked an artery in her groin during a simple test. But now we could hear her screams as we came out of the elevator on her floor. A nurse greeted us with the news that something had gone wrong after the surgery and two interns were now working on what was left of her leg to correct it. The worst part was that they did not want to give painkillers to anyone with so little body weight. It sounded as though they were torturing her to death.

I may not have been the bravest person in the world with medical emergencies, but I kept my head and insisted that my mother get the primary surgeon on the phone and request any and all drugs possible to alleviate her sister's suffering. The reason I made *her* call was because I could tell that the doctor had been impressed by Mother's charms and would give us immediate action.

While waiting for the medication, I watched my mother gently caress her sister's brow. It particularly stuck in my mind since it was an uncharacteristic thing for her to do.

After Mother had returned back home, my aunt insisted on showing me what was left of her leg because she feared that they had taken off more than they had told her they would. I tried to reassure her as best I could before I excused myself to go sit in the bathroom with my head between my legs so as not to pass out.

The next day when I went back to the hospital my aunt confided to me that the only thing she remembered clearly about the terrible day of the operation was the comfort she had felt when my mother had caressed her forehead.

It was a lesson I never forgot.

Years later, while still not able to acknowledge the reality of our mortality, I knew that I was the only person present to give my eighty-five-year-old father any comfort during his last two weeks of life in an intensive care unit. The doctors had tried their best but were not able to stop an ulcer in his stomach from bleeding. Now, one by one, his vital organs were shutting down.

On one of my visits, the doctors told me that my father was no longer conscious. But when I entered his cubicle the nurse who stayed by his bedside said that every time I walked in the room, his vital signs reacted sharply to my presence.

That day he seemed agitated and uncomfortable so

I asked him to move the index finger of his right hand in mine if he was in any pain or discomfort. I didn't have to wait long to feel his finger move ever so slightly in my hand. Within minutes I sent word to the doctors that I *could* communicate with my father and that he *was* in physical distress.

After that, I took nothing for granted and made sure each time I saw him that I held his hand, stroked his arm and told him how much he was loved. I even said that I was sure that Mother, who had died fifteen years before, was watching over him. I thought he would like that.

I did everything in my power to comfort him until the final moments of his life, when I went into complete denial of the fact that he was dying and left the hospital. I was at dinner with friends when I got the message that my father had passed away an hour after I had left him.

I know that I could have been riddled with guilt for having deserted him at the end. But I later accepted the fact that I had done the best I could to let him know that he was not alone. And no matter what condition he was in, he had been able to feel the touch of my hand and communicate—even if it was with only the slightest of movements of one finger.

At least I was beginning to "get it right."

When AIDS came along, it was considered a twentieth-century plague. The unknown factors of the disease frightened everyone—including the medical profession. Some even believed it was transmitted through the air. They believed you could catch it by just being in the same room with a patient. When a popular cabaret singer with AIDS was asked to talk about the disease on television, the crew insisted that he be confined behind a glass wall. I can only imagine how that must have made him feel.

The ramifications of a sick person's being so completely isolated by society are devastating. This means that there will be no one to hold your hand, give you a hug, or comfort you as you approach your final days—alone and afraid.

A hug or the human touch is not a danger with AIDS or most other diseases. The only thing society should fear is not having enough love to comfort someone in their agony so that they can leave this world with a feeling of peace.

One of our young men at the hospice had been offered a trip to Lourdes and was still strong enough to make the trip. The only visible sign of AIDS was the cancer on his face, which he managed to hide effectively with a special makeup.

My real purpose at the hospice became clear to me on the morning of his departure, when he said, "Tony, the real work you do at Gift of Love is not cleaning or mopping, but talking to me, touching Donald's shoulder as he walks by, or listening to Herbert—the little things that show you care about us."

It was never too much trouble to go up and down the stairs one more time to make sure everyone was comfortable. And sometimes it took a little ingenuity to figure out a new way to move someone and cause the least amount of pain or how to painstakingly clean a man who had such constant diarrhea that his rectum looked as though it had been split wide open into one big wound.

It was a shock the first time I saw that kind of devastation on a patient—something that no amount of painkillers could effectively help. The poor man would start to cry whenever he felt his next bowel movement coming on because he dreaded having to endure the cleaning process. I finally devised a way to wash him with a gentle antiseptic lotion that almost seemed to have a numbing effect on his affected part. The whole time I kept reassuring him in a soothing voice that I would go slowly and for him to let me know the moment he felt too much discomfort. In time he stopped dreading the procedure because he trusted me to be as careful as possible. What I did was mentally put myself in his position and work with the same gentle touch I would have wanted for myself.

Mario was another man who needed more than painkillers to get him through some rough moments. All day long, every fifteen to twenty minutes, he suffered from general spasms of pain throughout his whole body. The only thing that got him through it was for me to run to his bedside from wherever I might be in the house, and let him hang onto my hand until the spasms had passed. The pain only lasted a couple of minutes so I told him that every time he cried out I would be there for him to hang onto until it passed. I eventually understood that, for Mario, my hand was the most effective painkiller we had in the house. And I never let him down.

When Wendell was days away from death, I overheard him on the phone, begging his mother in Tennessee to come and visit him before he died. I could see by his face that his efforts had been in vain.

I then went to one of the Sisters and told her what I had heard and that if it was a question of money, I would be happy to pay for her trip.

Sister sadly shook her head and said, "Tony, I'm sorry to say, but money is not the problem."

All I could do was go up to Wendell's room and see if he was all right. As soon as he saw me, he said, "Would you give me a hug? Sometimes that's the best medicine."

I understood that sometimes it was the *only* medicine.

It had taken me the better part of a lifetime to erase the fear of being fully present at the passing of a loved one or a friend, but the gifts they gave back to me were much more than I could ever have given them.

And all I needed was my two hands.

Sometimes touch can not only help someone who is ill or dying but can also help someone such as a homeless person who is living on the street in desperate circumstances. The saddest part is that many of these people, through no fault of their own, have been reduced to begging for shelter or a piece of bread and are shunned and ignored as though they were lepers.

On a beautiful Spring day in 2013 I was walking down Madison Avenue in New York when, because of a neurological disease doctors say I inherited from my mother, I found it increasingly difficult for my legs to go much farther without resting somewhere for a few moments. I had just reached the steps of a church where an elderly black lady was sitting with a cup for money at her feet. Not only was she elderly but her whole body was severely crippled with arthritis. I also noticed that, although she had a smile that could light up the Empire State Building, she did not have a tooth left in her mouth.

When I leaned down and asked if I could sit next to her, she replied in a soft voice with the hint of a southern drawl, "Of course you can, Honey."

She seemed so friendly that I introduced myself and said, "My name's Tony. What's yours?"

She smiled at this complete stranger and said that her name was Muzette.

"What a beautiful name," I replied.

"Thank you," said my new friend, and added, "My mother's name was Muzette and my daughter's name is Muzette."

"Do you have a place to sleep, Muzette?"

"Oh, yes, I have a little place on West 97th Street, but I'm here because I don't have enough money to eat."

My mind couldn't help but think of the wonderful and expensive dinner my partner (and by then spouse) of forty-eight years, Jim Russo, and I were going to give as a birthday celebration that night at La Grenouille restaurant for a very privileged and very rich lady. All I wanted at that moment was to make sure that Muzette with the beautiful smile had a lovely dinner also, so I took a twenty dollar bill out of my pocket, crumpled it up and put it in my new friend's severely crippled hand.

Without even looking at what I had put in her hand, she put it in her purse and asked, "Honey, can I have a hug?"

All I can say is that it was one of the warmest and best hugs I have ever had in my life. We then laughed together when I said (I was dressed in full Versace), "You know Muzette, we must really look like the Odd Couple!"

While we quietly sat and watched the parade of Upper East Side elite make their way to stores such as Chanel or Ralph Lauren, this wise woman who refused to let her life's circumstances defeat her spirit turned to me and said, "You know Tony, many of these people are much poorer than I am."

I could only think, What a remarkable and inspiring human being I have the privilege of sitting next to on the steps of this church.

When my legs felt rested and it was time for me to get home, Muzette gave me another one of her magical hugs, and when I reached the corner of the street and turned back to see her, she blew me a kiss.

Of course I couldn't wait to tell Jim the moment I walked in the door about the remarkable angel I had met that afternoon.

Later that night at the restaurant I told my wealthy friend about my encounter with Muzette and that instead of buying her an expensive birthday present I had given her "present" (the twenty dollars) to Muzette so she could have a nice dinner that night too.

About a week after my extraordinary and inspiring encounter with Muzette, Jim was making his way down Madison Avenue when he saw a little black lady in a wheelchair holding a cup with a couple of dollars in it in her twisted hands. He thought nothing of it until he got halfway down the street and turned back to ask her, "Are you Muzette?"

"Why, yes. How did you know?"

"I'm a friend of Tony's. He told me all about you and said that you are his angel!"

"But he's MY angel!" she replied.

Jim could hardly wait to come home and tell me the good news. He had met my Muzette and in his eyes and heart he could also tell that she *was* an angel.

A few days after Jim met Muzette, I was again walking up Madison Avenue when I heard someone call out to me. There was my angel sitting in her wheelchair with her arms out ready to give me a hug.

Her first words to me were, "I met your hubby the other day."

She smiled and laughed as we talked and I realized that she remembered every word of the conversation we had had on the steps of the church the first day we met. That, of course called for another of her magical hugs.

As soon as I was ready to go on my way, I noticed a homeless man on the other side of the street. His legs were obviously handicapped as he stumbled, half hopping on one leg through the traffic to get to us.

I don't know what I was expecting when he miraculously reached the street corner where Muzette was giving me a farewell hug, but I will never forget the words he shyly spoke as he came closer to me.

"Can I have a hug too?" he asked. And that was all he wanted.

CHAPTER 4

Music

"Take My Hand, Precious Lord"

Ever since I can remember, music has played a large role in my life. When I was a child the radio was always on, and later, when I discovered records, *they* became my passion. I told my family that someday I would either become a singer or be a missionary. I wasn't religious but I kind of liked the idea of helping other people. At the time I didn't realize that music and helping others were not mutually exclusive.

It was no surprise that after graduating from high school, I went into show business. Musical comedy, concerts, and cabaret became my life. And in 1984 the couturier Pierre Cardin, who was a driving force in show business in Europe, brought me to Paris to introduce me at a gala in my honor at Maxim's. I then stayed and worked in Europe for ten years doing recordings and concerts.

During those years I occasionally came back to the United States for a job that interested me; but more importantly, Mother Teresa showed me that any musical ability I had could also be used within the confines of her homes for the dying—and give me more satisfaction than I could have ever imagined.

• • •

During my first week at Gift of Love, I met a patient by the name of James who was not only unable to coordinate his legs and arms but also could no longer articulate his words. He could make sounds but could not make himself understood. He had also lost his sight. This inability to communicate made it impossible for him to share his pain and fear with the other patients, the Sisters, or the volunteers.

My heart broke every time I saw him lying on the couch in the lounge, locked within his own body. So every time I passed Mother Teresa's picture on the wall next to the chapel door, I prayed for some kind of guidance—some small way to unlock the door of his isolation.

Suddenly I felt inspired to run up the stairs, pull up a stool, and say, "James, why don't we sing?"

Seeing a flicker of interest on his face, I took his hand and started to sing an old spiritual called "His Eye Is on the Sparrow." Before I had finished the first line, the most extraordinary smile lit up his face. He then grabbed my hand with all his strength and started to sing along. Of course, he was only making sounds, but I could tell that he knew it perfectly and was singing every word along with me. We sang it twice and I'm sure he could have happily gone on for hours. I walked away in awe that something I had taken for granted my whole life could make such a difference in someone else's life. I also learned that the simple gift of music can bring joy, no matter what the human condition.

Another thing I learned that day was that the Sisters noticed everything that went on in the house.

Shortly after breakfast I was mopping the kitchen floor (I have friends who would kill for a picture of that), when a Sister came up to me with a sweet smile on her face and said, "Tony, you never mopped or swept a floor before you came here, did you?"

"Does it really show, Sister?"

She then laughed and apologized, thinking maybe she'd been rude.

I said, "No, Sister, I *pay* people to do this for *me.*"

After I assured her that she had not hurt my feelings, she asked, "What do you do?"

"I'm a singer."

Never one to miss an opportunity, she said, "Oh, well, then you must sing for the men at lunch."

When lunchtime came around I thought she might have forgotten about it, but as soon as the patients were served, she announced, "Now, Tony, you can sing!" I figured the hit song of the day had been "His Eye Is on the Sparrow," so I did it again for everyone else. Not only was James smiling and rocking back and forth, but the other guys were enjoying the entertainment too. I thought, "Wow, I don't need an orchestra, a piano, or a theater to give people pleasure. I can do it anywhere!"

The most satisfying of all, though, was when I discovered the physical and emotional peace my singing could bring to someone in the last days of their life. The effect of a soft, continuous rendition, rather like a mantra, of a song such as "Take My Hand, Precious Lord" never ceased to amaze me. Bodies rigid with pain relaxed. They no longer gasped for air, and the look of fear was erased from their faces. The beauty of it is that you don't need to be a professional or have a great voice. My mother, who had no singing voice at all, could make me feel loved and protected at bedtime with any silly song that popped into her head. It's something anybody can do. And there are no rules.

There were also times when I least expected it that music created its own miracle—times when it was the only option left to me in a situation where I felt woefully inadequate and lost.

It seemed that every day that I walked into Gift of Love I was forced to face a new problem that made me want to put my coat back on and walk out. But I never did. I don't know why I stayed, except that the rewards I derived from facing the constant challenges of life and death were stronger than my insecurities and fears.

One of my greatest challenges was a black man called Sada who had been raised in a French-African nation. Sada was suffering from a whole gamut of AIDS-related problems. He knew he was going to die soon and he wanted to get it over with.

The first morning I met Sada, I saw that the Sisters were bathing him—a task they usually left to a volunteer. I then went down to the kitchen, where the night volunteer told me that Sada only allowed the Sisters to care for him. If a volunteer tried to help, he would throw anything within his reach, such as a bedpan, a urinal, or a bowl of porridge. He would also try to bite any of us who came too close to him.

I wasn't really concerned about Sada until twelve o'clock noon rolled around, the time when the Sisters went down to the convent for a couple of hours every day.

Before leaving me alone to care for the patients, one of the Sisters said, "Tony, Sada didn't eat his breakfast this morning. Would you please make him a full bowl of Cream of Wheat with a little butter and salt? That's the way he likes it. And also a bowl of grapes which he will peel himself with his teeth. Make sure there are enough pillows under his head so that you can first place one bowl and then the other in the crook of his arm. After that he can feed himself. Oh, and be sure to give him a little plastic bag for him to spit out the parts of the grapes that he doesn't want to eat."

I'm sure I stared at the outside of the convent door for a good five minutes after she left, hoping that she would soon reappear and tell me it was just a joke. But it wasn't. Once again the Sisters had left me to fend for myself as best I could.

Seeing that I was the only volunteer for the day, I prepared Sada's meal, put it on a tray, and took it upstairs to his room, where he was lying in bed facing the wall.

I put the tray down on the hospital table behind his back and said, "Sada, I have some Cream of Wheat and some grapes for you." There was no response, so I went around the bed, where there was a space of no more than a foot between him and the wall. I could see his eyes were open and void of expression.

Since I was getting no response and dared not venture any closer, I told him, "The food is on the table and you can have it any time you want."

There was still no reaction, so I went back around to the other side of the bed where the food was sitting on the table, and softly sang "Take My Hand, Precious Lord." Then I left the room.

A few minutes later I came back and was surprised to see that he had turned around, was facing the food, and looked ready to eat. I carefully approached him and gave him the food the way the Sisters had told me to. By then Sada no longer seemed wary of me and let me know how he wanted things done by pointing.

Sada must have weighed no more than sixty pounds, but he ate every mouthful.

I continued to check on him during the day and prayed he would not need a diaper change. I didn't want to push my luck too far. It probably would have taken an aria to prepare him for something like *that*.

In retrospect, I believe that the calm, loving influence of that simple song changed Sada's attitude and made him comfortable enough to accept the help I offered him that day.

In one way or another it seems to work for everyone. Some doctors say that hearing is the last of our senses to go at the time of death. Therefore it makes sense that soothing music would have the greatest influence on us as we prepare to leave this world. It's the last thing we can connect with, and I hope the first thing I hear after I have passed over.

CHAPTER 5

Respect

"Thank God it was you!"

The most precious gift we can give another human being who is in the last stages of life is respect. Whatever their condition, I am sure that on some level they are aware when their human dignity is being violated—especially in a hospital where the staff is often overworked and underpaid. This is why every patient needs an advocate who cares enough to fight for their rights when they are no longer able to. Even when their mental faculties are intact they are still the vulnerable ones in that bed, often afraid to ask questions in case they will be made to suffer for being a "bother."

Many of my affluent friends have the luxury of prominent doctors and surgeons, important hierarchy in the medical world, who are prepared to cater to their every need. But these friends are in the minority. Most people have to deal with the cards they are dealt and become understandably intimidated when confronted by a person in a uniform who controls the comfort of their every waking moment.

Even my friend Ethel Merman, a show business legend for fifty-five years, was on occasion subject to unnecessary pain while she lay dying at home of a brain tumor.

. . .

One morning she had annoyed her nurse when she complained at length that some of her jewelry was missing. Later in the day, when she told the nurse that she was uncomfortable and needed an enema, the nurse took the opportunity to come back at her with, "Why? Do you think you'll find your jewelry up there?"

I was pleased to hear that Ethel was still able to unleash a few choice words back at the nurse. But not long after that episode she began to lose the ability to speak and was no longer able to defend herself. Fortunately, her son, Bob, stayed at her side for the ten long months it took her to die. He was one person I know who was able to "get it right." Bob was present to monitor every aspect of his mother's care and to comfort her in her final days as she lay mute and unable to move on the hospital bed he had had installed in her bedroom.

Joseph was twenty-six years old when he came to Gift of Love, and had one of the sharpest minds I had ever known. Although he looked quite healthy, he told me that in all probability he would not live more than a year. There was nothing maudlin about it—just a fact—a fact that proved to be eerily accurate.

In that year, however, we had some great times going for walks around the neighborhood, talking about his experiences as an adventurous young man who loved the rock group The Grateful Dead (something I knew nothing about). He was also unapologetically gay and was not going to be anything but himself whether it pleased his family or not. His courage and grace in the face of dcath was awe-inspiring. He feared no one and loved his family whether they approved of him or not.

One afternoon while the Sisters were down in the convent, I took Joseph into the pharmacy to give him his medication. He was sitting down waiting for his pills, when without any warning he started to retch. I had just enough time to reach for the wastebasket for him to throw up in, but could do nothing about the diarrhea that was flowing down his legs and out of the bottom of the tracksuit he was wearing. There was nothing I could do but hold the wastebasket and pray.

I'm sure this violent attack only *seemed* to go on forever. But once it ended, Joseph was not concerned with the terrible things that had just happened to his body. He was only embarrassed at the mess he had created for me to clean up.

As soon as he was well enough I half carried him upstairs, trailing diarrhea all the way. Then I helped him take off his clothes, and put him in the shower.

The whole time I kept reassuring him that it was all right. There was nothing to feel embarrassed about. We were friends and had to deal with the good as well as the bad. Tomorrow we'd find something fun to do and forget about this. It didn't mean a thing. I was just sorry he had had to endure this painful experience.

As for the soiled tracksuit he had been wearing, he begged, "Please, Tony, throw it out. I never want to see it again." Since I knew how thrifty the nuns were with their unyielding vow of poverty, and was sure that they would never approve of my throwing a perfectly good tracksuit away, I wrapped the clothes up and discarded them where *no one* would ever see them again.

Whatever made Joseph comfortable about himself was all I cared about. And he knew I meant it when I told him that the vomit and diarrhea didn't matter. I respected the intelligent, generous, and funny guy I considered my friend, no matter what awful things happened to his physical self.

I knew he understood when I heard him say, "Thank God it was you, Tony. Thank God it was you."

At Gift of Love, I found that AIDS was often accompanied by dementia, a mental condition which gives some caregivers the erroneous impression that the patient is no longer cognizant of their human dignity.

On my first day at the hospice I met a man called Sam, who, on the outside, appeared quite healthy. I did not yet know about dementia and wondered why I could never make any sense out of what he was saying. I could see that he was an affable fellow, but he kept repeating the same inane things over and over.

The next day one of the Sisters asked me to accompany Sam to the clinic for an appointment with a neurologist. He wanted to go alone, but Sister insisted that I go with him since he usually got lost. Not only was this my first time in a Medicaid clinic, but I had no idea as to the extent of Sam's mental deterioration.

Sam's appointment was for 1:00 P.M. but it soon dawned on me that *everyone's* appointment was for 1:00 P.M. You went in to see the doctor according to what time you arrived.

While waiting, I tried to evaluate Sam's cognitive abilities. As we conversed, I understood nothing he said and could only react in whatever way seemed appropriate at the time. He kept pointing to his legs and saying, "Well, this is ahr, ahr, ahr," and "Well, that's the way it goes." Then he would laugh. So I would answer, "That's the way it goes," and laugh with him. We did this over and over.

Sam and I waited about an hour and a half at the hospital before the nurse called his name. A young woman doctor was waiting for us in the examining room.

When I discreetly asked what his neurological problems stemmed from, she told me there was no way of knowing the exact cause of Sam's mental impairment, but that he had had a stroke, possibly caused by IV drug use, which had sent an infection to his brain.

She added, "All of this has destroyed the receiver part of his brain, so whatever you tell him doesn't get through. The only thing Sam goes by is the tone of your voice and your expression."

In order to illustrate her point, she stood in front of him, and with a big smile on her face said, " Sam, you're a silly goose!"—and laughed right in his face.

I don't care how much of Sam's brain she may have thought had been damaged, he knew intuitively that he was not being respected.

Sam's mood immediately darkened. Something was terribly wrong and he was not quite sure what it was. I wanted to tell her that *she* was the silly goose. This doctor had no idea of the storm that was brewing as she dismissed us.

Once we got outside her office, Sam was in a rage. He knew that he had been insulted and sat down in the lobby crying out, "She don't know what—what—where— What're they doing?— What is this shit? —See this?— What is?— What're, what're, what're you going to do, huh?"

I gave him time to vent his frustrations before I knelt in front of him and calmly said, "Come on, Sam. Let's go home now." Then, like a child, he slowly got up and followed me into the street.

The next morning the Sisters were surprised that Sam, who usually gave them a hard time over taking his medications, popped them right in his mouth. A little while later I was sweating in a tiny, unventilated room washing the breakfast dishes by hand when Sam came around the corner with a big grin on his face. He opened his hand, showed me the soggy pills he had taken out of his mouth when the Sisters weren't looking, popped them back into his mouth, swallowed them, grabbed my arm and said, "You're O.K." Then I knew that no matter what his brain function may have been, he understood that he had a friend.

Each time that I took Sam to the hospital for another appointment (I made sure we never saw that same neurologist again), the Sisters told me how pleased they were with the way Sam and I got along. But getting along with Sam was not as complicated as it might seem. All I did was treat him with the same respect as I would anybody else, and he responded in kind.

Eventually the Sisters, fearing Sam's increasingly violent outbursts towards them, the other patients, and volunteers, felt they had no choice but to send him to the psychiatric ward of the hospital to spend the remainder of his days.

As for me, I was saddened to see him leave us. He had never given me any reason to fear him, and my friendship with him was no less meaningful because of his mental impairment. I can say that if I enriched his life in any way, he certainly enriched mine, and taught me the importance of respecting all human beings, whether they are totally lucid, in the throes of dementia, or in a coma.

CHAPTER 6

Never Assume Anything

"Please don't ever stop doing what you're doing."

Whenever someone is dying we must be prepared for a new and unexpected experience every day. Complacency usually creates a false sense of security and can backfire when you least expect it. The first person to teach me that lesson was my aunt Tata, who spent the last three months of her life in the hospital dying of a cancer that had spread throughout her body.

I went to see Tata every day and did not really want to admit to myself how much she counted upon my daily visits. On a beautiful summer afternoon I was walking towards the hospital when I told myself that I just didn't feel like going that day. I mulled the question over in my mind while nearing the entrance and decided, "Oh what the heck, I'll just go in for a few minutes, make some small talk, and leave."

The minute I entered her private room she sat up in bed and cried, "Thank God, you're here. I've been praying for you to come. Your mother was here earlier and I didn't dare tell her that I have no recollection of why I'm in the hospital. The only person I trust to admit it to is you. I've been frantic ever since she came by this morning. But I knew I could tell you without your thinking I was crazy."

Somehow the cancer, which had metastasized to her brain, had short-circuited her memory, and the only person she was comfortable to share her confusion with was me. My problem then was to find something to say that would not make her more uncomfortable or frightened.

I quickly decided that a full disclosure of her condition would not be necessary at that time. My immediate course of action was to tell her that she had a problem with her lungs. I added that the doctors had feared tuberculosis but had ruled it out, before I moved on to the subject she seemed most worried about.

I assured her that her memory loss was only temporary (which turned out to be true)—that it was due to the fact that she had lost so much weight and had become anemic. As soon as they got enough nourishment into her body her mind would be fine.

After I convinced Tata that she had nothing to worry about and that her memory would soon return, she fell back against her pillows with a sigh of relief.

My lesson for that day was never to think that just because everything had gone smoothly up until then, this would be a crisis-free day. When someone is critically ill, there are no guarantees that things will be the same from moment to moment. One has to learn how to cope with each situation as it comes along.

My philosophy is also to lie as little as possible. You usually know instinctively how much a loved one is ready to hear and in what form they are ready to hear it.

The subject is not that different from answering a child's first questions about sex. You know your own children, what stage they are at, and what kind of information they are able to assimilate at that time. Sometimes you have to (as I call it) "tap dance around the bed" for a while, but the clues, in time, will all be given to you.

My only advice is never to assume anything. One hour or one day before, I may not have been as desperately needed at Tata's side. But that day the whole picture had changed and I was the only person in her life who could offer the kind of comfort she required. I hate to think of the mental anguish she would have had to endure on one of the last days of her life, had I assumed she didn't need me that afternoon and not continued on my way to her hospital room for a "quick Hello."

Little did I know that the first time I would use my voice and my presence to ease the fear of another human being in an end-of-life crisis would be to help my step-grandfather, whom I called "Grand-père," when I was twelve years old.

He was married to my paternal grandmother (a difficult woman at best), and had been a doctor in the French army fighting in the Boxer Rebellion. He was eighty-four years old and had a serious heart condition, something that could not be treated as effectively in 1953 as it can today. He had also been decorated many times by the government and was revered as a retired General.

One evening while we were dining at my grandmother's château, he suddenly announced to us all—

including his son, who was his physician—that there was a serious problem developing in his heart. Since the General had been a doctor himself, everyone knew that the obvious fear on his face was not to be taken lightly.

For reasons I will never understand, the next thing I knew, my mother, father, uncle and I were soon on our way to Angers, which was only three kilometers away, so my uncle could get the medicine his father needed from his office. On the way, my mother, in her inimitable fashion, was already preparing for the worst by telling everyone that I was too young to go to a funeral. I'm sure that she was already counting on the fact that she had not forgotten to bring a black dress from New York in case of a death in the family. That was my mother—always prepared for any and every eventuality.

Being a sensitive young man, I was strongly affected by the fear I saw on my step-grandfather's face at the dinner table and even more so when we returned with the medications and saw him lying in his bedroom, which happened to be next to mine. My feelings of anxiety at his obvious distress were evident to my grandmother as I walked to his bed to try and reassure him as best as a twelve-year-old could.

It was then that my grandmother suggested that I recite a poem for her husband. Of course, both he and I strongly objected to such an absurd idea.

"Why on earth should you make the boy recite a poem at a time like this?" said the General, with the very evident fear still on his face.

I also told her I thought it a very foolish idea until,

undeterred by our mutual protestations, she pulled out a book of poems and pointed to the selection I was to read. It was called *"La Vierge à la Crèche,"* by Alphonse Daudet.

It was about the Virgin Mary cradling her baby Jesus and singing softly while waiting for him to fall asleep. The child laughed and waved his arms happily at the sound of her voice, which made his mother sad, very sad that her baby Jesus would not close his eyes.

She cried, "Sleep, my little lamb, my beautiful white lamb. Sleep, it's late, the lamp has gone out. Sleep my love, and sleep without worry." But baby Jesus lay awake in her arms.

"It's cold, the wind is blowing and we have no more fire. Sleep, it is nighttime, the night of the Good Lord. Quick, my darling, close your eyes." But the infant Jesus still would not sleep.

"If you sleep for just a while your dreams will come like a bird in flight and build a nest over your eyes. They'll come; sleep; my gentle Jesus." Alas, in spite of the Blessed Mother's songs and prayers said in vain, her Baby Jesus still would not sleep.

And the Virgin Mary, her eyes misty with unshed tears, leaned close to her beloved child and wept, "You're still not sleeping, your mother is weeping, your mother is weeping my little love…"

As her tears fell on the little child, Baby Jesus closed his eyes and fell fast asleep.

When I finished reading this beautiful poem to Grand-père, I saw the tears coming down his cheeks. The poem had done its magic. All I could do was kiss him on his wet cheeks and say goodnight. Something such as the poem that neither of us wanted had allowed the angels to do their job well and take the fear away from his face. Neither of us could have asked for more.

Grand-père was a great intellectual who retired to his library/study every afternoon after lunch. The room was filled with priceless books he had collected during his lifetime. The day after I had read the poem to him, he made his way to his precious library, picked out a very old and beautiful leather-bound book of poems that he inscribed to me, "With great love from your grandfather."

How wonderful it is to look back and be grateful that in the end we did not assume that reading the poem might be a silly thing to do, and gave him the chance to transform his fear into a wonderful feeling of love and peace.

I discovered that when someone is nearing the end of their life and the truth of their condition is suddenly made clear to them, one can never assume where the unexpected blessing that will ease the fear and give them comfort will come from.

Every one of the lessons I learned as I went through life was carefully filed away in my mind—both the times I got it right and when I didn't. I learned from them all. And they all came in handy when I had to deal with a dozen cases every day at Gift of Love.

. . .

Even though most of the patients at Gift of Love came from varied backgrounds, I quickly learned not to make any assumptions about any of them either.

On my first day of work I waited in the lounge while Wendell went into the bathroom to attach a colostomy bag to his abdomen. He was an emaciated young man whose body was covered in Kaposi's sarcoma (a type of cancer particularly associated with AIDS). I understood that he had had the colostomy because the cancer had spread to his inner organs.

I didn't yet know how he felt about this new volunteer called Tony who had just entered their midst, but since he had seemed friendly from the start, I thought he might enjoy sitting around and having a chat.

Wendell seemed genuinely pleased to see me "hanging out" on the couch and immediately launched into the story of his life.

When we first met I could tell that he had above average intelligence, and assumed that he had had a higher education. I don't know where his impressive command of the English language came from, but within minutes I learned to put away all preconceived notions I had had about his background or education before hearing his story.

He told me that he had been born in Tennessee to a family that could never have been mistaken for "The Brady Bunch." His home situation was so intolerable that he ran away to New York City at the age of thirteen and became a transvestite prostitute in order to support himself. He also worked in drag shows, impersonating Barbra Streisand and Ann-Margret. At twenty-six, he was now in the last stages of AIDS.

I could discern no self-pity as I sat and listened to the saga of his short and tragic life. There was just a need to share a part of himself with someone he felt he could trust.

That day my lesson was never to take anyone's outer demeanor or way of expressing themselves as an indication of their life story. And we remained friends until his death four months later.

Donald was the opposite from Wendell. He was an older black man who gave the appearance of any homeless person one might run into on the streets of New York.

The day before leaving for a month in Paris to work on a new CD, I stopped by the lounge and saw Donald reading a book about saints and martyrs.

"Donald, I don't understand why these saints had to become martyrs—wear hair shirts, flagellate themselves, and fast. Why did they have to make themselves suffer? Isn't there enough suffering in the world without creating more for ourselves?"

"Oh, Tony, each minute of every day I could scream in anger at what is happening to my life and my body, but I don't. I realize each one of us is carrying our own cross, no matter who we are."

I thought, "Wow, this man expresses himself beautifully!"

When he asked me where I was going, I answered, "Paris."

"Oh, what do you do in Paris?"

"I sing there."

"That's interesting. When I was in Paris I knew Hazel Scott and Charlie Bird."

He had just named two legendary musicians, so I asked what he had been doing in Paris and had he been in show business.

He answered, "No, I was a student."

Then he started talking about how the world perceives the French as having an attitude. He added, "Arrogant is the word. The French arrogance. After all, what do you expect when you have someone like Louis the Fifteenth, who says, '*Après nous le déluge.*' You know they all have a certain frame of mind and everything is *de rigueur.*"

I was sitting up a little straighter as we discussed the homeless situation and words like "largesse" rolled effortlessly off his tongue. No matter if I agreed with his views of life or not, I never felt that any of his conversation was for effect. The words all came naturally. And once more I found that you can never judge by appearances.

Because I allowed Donald to dispel my immediate judgment of his intellect and worldly experience, I was able to share so much more with him at the end of his life—a sharing which enriched both his life and mine.

. . .

Another patient who expressed himself well was a good looking, well-built young man called Ted. He was a recovering drug addict who had recently been diagnosed with AIDS while in prison. Besides dealing with his own terminal illness, he couldn't bear the thought of having passed the disease on to his younger brother by sharing needles. They had always been very close and now his sibling was sitting in prison in Comstock, New York, afraid to be tested. I realized there were no magic answers—all I could do was listen.

The first day I met Ted, he was so anguished and confused that I thought he should write his feelings down. It seemed to me like a good way to sort out his pain. Something, however, kept me from suggesting it to him.

The idea was still in my head the day he told me he wanted to send a new pair of sneakers to his brother in prison. He then asked me if I would write the address on the package. I thought it might be because he was too weak to do it himself, but instead he admitted that it was because "I don't know how to write."

Someone must have been whispering in my ear all that time and telling me to mind my own business!

After getting past the assumptions about how he could deal with his terminal illness, I got to know more about the *real* Ted and was able to search for appropriate ways to allay his fears and anxiety.

I was also grateful that Ted had a lovely girlfriend

who helped me take care of him during the last weeks of his life. The morning he died, she came to the hospice, put her arms around me, and said, "Please, don't ever stop what you're doing."

No matter how many surprises I had at Gift of Love, there always came a time when I momentarily fell into the old trap of judging people by what they looked like. But over time, Gift of Love gave me the opportunity to discover how misguided I could be when I judged someone on the basis of a quick assessment I might have made as I passed them on the street.

After a particularly trying day at the clinic with James, who had lost the use of his arms and legs, his speech and his sight, the driver and I wheeled him into the back of the ambulette. The driver then told me to get into the passenger seat while he went back into the hospital for some paperwork. When I got in and turned around to see if James was all right, I noticed two seedy-looking characters who looked like homeless drug addicts seated behind me. There was also a strong smell of liquor in the van.

James, who was oblivious to anything but his own deep distress, kept crying and attempting to say the only word that came easily to him, "NO! NO! NO!" over and over again.

While I was praying for the driver to come back soon in case I needed protection against these "shady" characters behind me, I saw one of them—who had never seen James before in his life—turn around, pat him on the knee, and with great concern and compassion in his voice, gently ask, "How're you doin', Buddy?"

It was hard to believe how frightened I had been by these men before witnessing this genuinely human gesture, which gave James momentary comfort from his suffering.

Peace is sometimes offered in unexpected disguises at the end of someone's life. We can never assume that we automatically have all the answers. The important thing is that when help *is* offered we just need to be open enough to recognize it and be grateful.

And I never had to do anything but sit quietly and learn my lesson.

CHAPTER 7

Helping Each Other

"Angels come in many forms."

I'll never know what the patients were like before we met at Gift of Love, but it was clear that the majority of them came from pretty rough backgrounds. A young man once told me that the only toys he had known as a child were the discarded syringes littering the floor of his mother's house.

By the time they came to us, they knew they were dying. Everyone was in the same position. And the burning question in each person's mind when someone died was "Am I next?"

In spite of their individual backgrounds, each one of the men showed a great understanding of their fellow human beings. And that's why I cared for them equally. Some were easier to get along with and some easier to talk to, but I could see something wonderful and good coming out in each of them. I saw evidence of it every day.

Whether they came from middleclass homes in the suburbs or from the ghettos of America, there was a grace that touched these men at the end of their lives and made them reach out to their "brothers" in the house. Instead of allowing bitterness to take over as their bodies failed, they rose above the pain and healed their spirits with incredible acts of generosity and love towards each other.

Basically one could say that this is the way we should live our lives even without the specter of death hovering over our heads. It was also one of the lessons Mother Teresa was so anxious for us all to learn.

One of the first men I met at the hospice who epitomized the spirit of love in action was a refined black man called Jimmy who—unlike most of the others—had no outward signs of AIDS. He was so intelligent and well spoken that I was surprised to hear that he had been a heroin addict for twenty-five years. During all that time he had held down a job loading trucks. The drugs had never gotten in his way, but he had needed a certain amount each day in order to function—not get high.

I admired the man I knew only as Jimmy—the man who was always there to help any of the others who was in a difficult situation. I like to believe that the gratification he received from his willingness to be of service to his fellow patients may have been one of the reasons he was able to successfully fight the disease for so long.

A perfect example of his unflinching dedication to his fellow man was the morning I walked into Wendell's room and found that not only had his urinal spilled on the floor but his colostomy bag had come loose and emptied all over the bed. This time Wendell was too ill to help me. I don't think he was even well enough to understand the extent of the damage that had taken place.

While I surveyed the disaster, I seriously considered

leaving the room, walking down the stairs, and out the front door. It seemed like too much for me to deal with.

That's when I turned around and saw Jimmy, my guardian angel, walk in. He already had a surgical mask on and was prepared to join me in battle. His calm presence was enough to keep me in the room.

Together, Jimmy and I cleaned up the floor and the bed before we attached a new bag to Wendell's abdomen. I have to admit that I was especially grateful for the moral support when I realized that I was looking into Wendell's intestines. Then we put several absorbent pads under him in case of any leakage. By the time we were through, Wendell had drifted off to sleep.

That was only one of the many times Jimmy came to my rescue. He was also there to help me whenever it came time to take a problematic patient for an appointment at the clinic. And if two men had appointments at different clinics, he always offered to take one or the other for me.

We once took a man who was in the late stages of dementia for X-rays. After the procedure, the hospital staff informed us that our young patient had had diarrhea all over the table. They then left us alone to clean it up. And through it all Jimmy never left my side.

Jimmy was one of the few patients strong enough to eventually leave Gift of Love. I never saw him again, but I am sure that his consideration for others was instrumental in his longtime survival. He was also a catalyst to inspire other men in his position to feel useful to the guys they called their "brothers" and to give them more of a reason to go on living by feeling that there was a purpose to their lives.

But then, doesn't everyone need to feel a purpose in their life? Whether you are terminally ill or in the best of health, what could be better for your wellbeing than to feel useful to humanity? All the sermons in the world don't mean a thing. Just see how good one simple act of generosity can make you feel—especially generosity of the spirit.

Kindness and caring come in all sorts of different wrappings. Sometimes it comes from strangers and sometimes it can come from your best friend. But best of all is when it comes when you least expect it.

I had only been at Gift of Love for a few days when the Sisters received a frantic call from the clinic at St. Clare's Hospital saying that James, who had gone for his appointment alone in an ambulette, had once again become distraught and wouldn't let anyone near him. The hospital asked if anyone he knew from Gift of Love could come over and calm him. Having no idea what I was getting myself into, I agreed to hop into a cab and see if I could be of any help.

The nurses seemed relieved when I arrived, and took me into a *tiny* room with a desk, a filing cabinet, and James, sitting in a chair hollering, "No! *No!* No! *No!*" They told me it was probably a psychotic episode, so I knelt down in front of him and told him who I was. But he wasn't listening—he could no longer hear. By then he had retreated into his own world.

The nurses then suggested tranquilizing him, but I

pointed out that if they couldn't even take his temperature, they sure as hell were not going to get a needle or
a pill in him. Besides, how was I going to get a sedated
James back to the house? It was a real Catch-22. The
other option was to admit him, but they couldn't put
him in the psychiatric ward, since his problem was
organically oriented, stemming from a tumor on the
brain and a stroke.

No one knew what to do with the situation, so I said,
"Let's just leave him alone for a while—nobody talk to
him, nobody try and make him do anything. Just leave him
be and see what happens." The nurses and doctors quickly
agreed and left us alone together in the little room.

A few moments later I saw the door quietly open, and
a policeman came in with a prisoner in shackles (many of
the prisoners with AIDS in New York City were treated in
that clinic). I had only seen this in the movies, and
watched in fascination while the officer undid the chains
on the man's hands, ankles, and waist. As soon as the prisoner was free, the policeman walked out of the room, leaving me alone with not only a psychotic man but also—for
all I knew—a serial killer. However, having been brought
up with unfailing good manners, I soon found myself chatting away with the prisoner, hoping he might think I was
too nice a guy to take hostage or strangle. My only thought
was, "I can't believe this is happening to me!"

After running out of small talk, there was no way we
could ignore James's cries. The prisoner seemed truly
concerned with James's plight, and knelt down in front
of him. Then in a steady, calm voice he told him every-

thing would be all right. He said that James and he both had the same problem, but that they were in the right place with the right people to take care of them.

Within a few minutes James slumped down in his chair. His body seemed to relax and the crisis was over.

Was it a special gift only one patient could give to another, or did James just give out from fatigue? I'll never know how it happened, nor does it matter, but I prefer to think that that man in shackles was sent by a higher power to help James that day, and in the process was able to do something positive for himself as well.

Angels come in many forms.

Not only did the staff get to know me well during my countless visits to St. Clare's Hospital with different patients, but I also found that the prisoners with AIDS got to know me as well. I would often see a dozen of them arrive together for their appointments at the clinic. They were unshackled as soon as they came in, and sat in the waiting room like anyone else. However, there was always at least one armed guard standing by.

These men and women may have been a "threat to society," but they always showed great concern whenever I came in with a distraught patient like James. They knew they could someday be in his condition or possibly even worse, and instead of hardening their hearts, they opened up to strangers like James and tried to comfort them. They also understood that I was not a miracle man. Therefore in giving their support to my patient they were also giving it to me.

I couldn't help but think of my proper Bostonian blueblooded mother the day a large group of shackled prisoners walked by me in the Emergency Room on their way to the clinic. As they passed by, I heard a friendly chorus of "Hi, Tony! How're you doin'?"

I think my mother would have gotten a kick out of looking down from heaven and seeing her son able to make friends in any part of our society. Actually, I believe that she *did* see me that day and was proud.

Whenever I think of St. Clare's Hospital I also remember Mark Bench, our friend in the Department of Social Services, a man I could call upon anytime we had a problem. Many's the time he went above and beyond the call of duty to see that our AIDS patients were properly taken care of. With Mark around, we never had to worry about our patients getting caught up in a web of hospital bureaucracy. He was never too busy to effectively take care of us in his calm and unassuming manner. I don't know what the patients, nuns, or I would have done without his support.

What I didn't know at the time was that Mark himself was dying of AIDS. It was something I learned only after his death. For me, his greatest legacy was the courage and compassion with which he touched the lives of so many other terminally ill patients.

Although Gift of Love was run by Catholic nuns, one subject that never became an issue was religion—a topic which has caused more wars than anything else I can think of in this world. To be honest, it was never an issue in any of Mother Teresa's hundreds of homes for the poor. Each person in her care was allowed their own beliefs, and when they died, they were buried accordingly. The only thing that could distress Mother Teresa was the thought that someone might not believe in some kind of God. She didn't care what you called your God or how you worshiped. She believed it was the same One who watches over us all. Her faith gave her her strength, and she wanted us to know the power and comfort it could be for everyone.

Every afternoon the men who wanted to or were strong enough would join together in the lounge for an hour or so of prayer. All religions were represented. It didn't matter if you were Christian, Jewish, Muslim or Hindu. Whatever you believed in was not threatened by a group of dying men gathered together in praise of whatever God they prayed to. And if someone believed in nothing, they were sometimes curious to come and see what it was all about.

The men all took turns praying for their families or a special loved one. But the part that moved me the most was when a man invariably chose to pray for another patient in the house who was going through an emotional crisis, or who was particularly suffering from the ravages of AIDS.

It was a powerful gift of physical and spiritual healing for every one of us in the room.

CHAPTER 8

Humor

"A very effective tool that costs nothing."

I doubt that I would have lasted one day, much less twelve years, working for Mother Teresa at Gift of Love or in Calcutta, if I had not been surrounded by people with a sense of humor. Not only did the nuns spread joy and laughter throughout the house, but it was Mother Teresa's not-so-secret weapon for bringing happiness to the poor and the dying. If one of her Sisters was looking gloomy, she refused to let her leave the convent that day. She thought those in need had enough troubles without a sad-faced nun in their midst.

The Sisters found laughter in as many ways as they found their joy. It was in the simple things of everyday life—the silly things that we might overlook while trying to impress everyone with our brilliance and charm. They had no agenda except the joy of living every moment of life.

Their humor was so infectious that the dying men in the house were more than happy to join in. How could the patients have the same focus on their sickness and pain when they were busy being a part of the laughter that surrounded them every day?

Doctors have also advocated laughter as an effective

medicine against infection and disease. There is no question that it is a comfort to anyone in any stage of their illness. It can also open up new lines of communication that were not possible before. How do we know that lighthearted banter is not uplifting to a patient in a coma? Why would they want to be surrounded by sadness? A depressive attitude around a sickbed does nothing positive for anyone. Even the caregivers need a way to release the pressures involved in attending to the needs of the dying. Or I should say *especially* the caregivers, since they are sometimes the key to the patients' attitude towards their illness.

This does not mean that we did not face the tragic realities of life and the specter of death that hovered over the house. But no one had to give their power over to it.

Most of the men were so young that they welcomed the opportunity to laugh every chance they had. They may have been dying of AIDS, but they were going to live on this earth and enjoy whatever they could while they were still here. And since some of them had never had a proper childhood, I always encouraged them to be silly and play the practical jokes they had not enjoyed as children.

Wilfredo was a bright, uneducated young man who had emigrated from San Salvador as a child, and for the last ten years he had worked carrying bottles up and down from the basement in a bar. Now, at Gift of Love, he was more than eager to express himself and let the kid emerge.

One morning, I was washing breakfast dishes in the tiny, windowless room with the three sinks: one to boil the dishes, one to wash them by hand with bleach and soap, and one to rinse them in. While sweating and working, I noticed that the lights kept mysteriously going off, leaving me in total darkness. I had no idea who was responsible until I saw a red sleeve slip inside the doorway, switch off the light, and then quickly disappear. The next time it happened, I ran into the hallway in time to catch Wilfredo, in his red jacket, running down the stairs, giggling and laughing like a little kid. He loved every moment of the big deal I made out of what I was going to do when I caught up with him.

I also suspected that Wilfredo was the instigator of the giggling that often took place during the afternoon hour of prayer in the lounge.

Roberto, a sweet little guy who in spite of a clubfoot ran all over the house carrying an IV that looked bigger than he did, started giggling every day while we prayed. When I later asked him what was so funny, he answered me in French (which *he* didn't speak) and I answered him in Spanish (which *I* didn't speak). So our silly conversation was hardly enlightening.

The next day when Roberto started a prayer, I saw Wilfredo, with an innocent look on his face, surreptitiously reach over, grab Roberto's foot, and tickle it. This time I don't believe that the Sisters were as amused as I was, but I loved the fact that these two could still act like the kids they had never had a chance to be.

. . .

Every two years each nun was transferred to another convent. The Superiors, however, with few exceptions, were only moved every five years. It made me sad each time a Sister had to leave us to go to another part of the world, because it meant that I might never again see someone I had worked closely with in countless life and death situations. The first four nuns who left us were the most meaningful to me, though, since they were the ones who initiated me into the ways of the house.

The first time a Sister I knew had to leave Gift of Love, I didn't realize it would be such an important occasion and that so many Missionaries of Charity from other convents in the city would descend upon us.

I was upstairs washing dishes (again) when one of the Sisters asked if I would please come downstairs to the entryway, where they had all gathered, so I could sing a song in honor of the departing nun.

I stood on the first landing and looked down at a sea of nuns, dressed in blue and white saris, all laughing and chattering away. After introducing me from below, the Superior asked me to sing "Freely, Freely."

I must have been quite a sight standing on the stairs at nine in the morning, wearing my apron and my yellow rubber dishwashing gloves, singing my little heart out for all of those smiling faces.

As the Sister was leaving, I watched the gaggle of blue and white saris fill up the street outside the house and squeeze into every available car to accompany her to the Bronx, where she would stay until her flight to Washington the next day. When they drove away, I looked up from the sidewalk and saw all the patients hanging out of the windows, happily waving goodbye. There was no sadness, only smiles for the good times and the laughs that this Sister had shared with them all. How I wish I had had a camera to photograph this extraordinary scene.

Judging by the laughter, no one would have believed that this was a home filled with dying men. Few people I know could find that much laughter and fun in simple everyday occurrences. Laughter and joy were the one *positive* infectious thing in that house. It was also one of its greatest blessings.

In our society we are inundated with violence and negativity every time we turn on the television, go to the movies, or see the videogames we allow our children to play. We mustn't forget that we have the option of being selective in our choice of entertainment. Sometimes I think Mother Teresa had the right idea when she said, "My tabernacle is my 'television.'" She preferred to commune with God rather than waste her life in pursuit of mindless entertainment. It was what sustained her and gave her the strength to follow her calling.

In spite of the harshness of the environment she worked in, Mother was never the dour and unyieldingly serious woman many people think of her as having been. Her sense of humor was one of the most powerful gifts she possessed.

She once wrote to me in a letter:

". . . Be kind, show kindness in your eyes, kindness in your smile. . . to all who suffer and are lonely, give always a happy smile."

And she didn't stop with just a smile. She also knew the healing power of laughter. It was one of the many tools she used in her homes for the sick and the dying throughout the world—a very effective tool that costs nothing.

CHAPTER 9

Doing Whatever You Have to Do

"Holy Moly! Holy Moly!"

—Ethel Merman

A few years before my beloved Aunt Tata died, she was in the hospital, where the doctors were attempting to determine why she had lost so much weight and appeared to be slowly fading away, a little more each day. It seemed to us all, as she lay in her bed not responding, that she had given up the struggle to live on and fight for her life.

I was with her every day, and saw the gradual decline, until she simply lay there, her eyes barely open when I entered the room.

One day when the cause seemed quite hopeless—the doctors had come up with few answers, if any—I felt the desperation to do anything I could to bring my Tata back to life.

It may have seemed silly to anyone else at the time, but I suddenly remembered how much she had always loved gossip. So I sat next to her on her bed and started to invent any sort of scandalous story I could think of that might jog some interest in her brain. All of her and my mother's friends were easy targets for my vivid imagination.

After a few minutes, her eyes began to open, and she was showing more than a little interest in the fascinating tales that I was making up as I went along. Before I knew it, she was—for the first time in ages—sitting up in bed, taking it all in, with eyes big as saucers. I even had ready answers for her questions about the details of the stories I was fabricating.

After I left Tata, my mother nearly fainted when Tata phoned her for the first time in a long while, and she heard her sister's voice say, "That Tony is *so* interesting!"

I will never understand quite why, but, miraculously, my Tata had come back to us.

Many years later, on April 7, 1983, Ethel Merman, the greatest star Broadway has ever known, was suddenly struck down by what turned out to be a devastating malignant brain tumor. She lay in her bed in Roosevelt Hospital, where she had worked as a volunteer every Wednesday for ten years, unable to speak or care for herself in any way. It was a terminal diagnosis which left her as helpless as a little child, with a brain that was completely cognizant of her limitations and the terrible things that were happening to her.

At this point, before the doctors had given her heavy doses of the steroid prednisone, which temporarily lessened the swelling in her brain so she could at least speak and walk with help, she could only lie in her hospital bed, facing a bleak and final illness that had taken away her life as she knew it in a heartbeat.

One day, as we often did, Jim Russo and I went to visit Ethel. We took with us the actress Carole Cook, someone we had introduced to Ethel in the 1970s. They had become fast friends over the years, so Carole flew from L.A. to New York to visit Ethel at Roosevelt Hospital with us.

When we walked into the room, Ethel was lying there, very much the way Tata had been. She hardly responded to our visit.

It was then—again—that, knowing how much Ethel loved gossip, as much as Tata did, I sat on her bed and began creating stories from my imagination about people we both knew. The gossip and scandalous stories came easily to me, because I knew so well what might stimulate Ethel's interest.

One fictitious story I can never forget was about the legendary singer the famous columnist Walter Winchell had dubbed the "Incomparable Hildegarde." Hildy, as her friends called her, had made a huge success in nightclubs and recordings around the world from the 1930s through the 1980s, when I worked with her.

A woman called Anna Sosenko had always taken the credit for having "created" Hildegarde and her legend, and for having written Hildegarde's signature song, "Darling, *Je Vous Aime Beaucoup.*"

Hildegarde and Anna had ended their relationship many years before I met them, and everyone speculated as to what had really occurred between them. So I decided to end the speculation for Ethel, who was still lying in a nonresponsive condition in her bed. My story for Ethel was that the two women had quarreled, until "Hildegarde punched Anna in the nose," effectively ending their long relationship.

By the time I reached the end of my story, Ethel was sitting up in bed, her eyes as big and wide open as Tata's had been, saying the only words she could still utter— "Holy Moly! Holy Moly!"

When I was through, and Jim, Carole and I finally left Ethel's hospital room, Carole turned to me and said, "That was amazing! I never knew those stories!"

To which I answered, "Neither did I. I just made them up!"

A few weeks later, when Ethel was home, with enough prednisone to temporarily give her back her ability to speak, I sometimes took old friends to her apartment in an effort to amuse our patient. However, one potentially embarrassing situation occurred on the day I took Hildegarde for a visit.

Ethel, who was delighted to see her, and still had a bit of the naughty little girl left in her, gave me a sly smile, with a meaningful twinkle in her eyes. Knowing Ethel as well as I did, I suddenly remembered the story I had made up in the hospital about Hildy and Anna's breakup. I was sweating bullets when I heard Ethel innocently say, "Oh, Hildy, I heard a story about you and Anna and the reason you ended your relationship. Someone told me that the two of you quarreled and you punched Anna in the nose."

I could tell by the little smile on her face that Ethel was thoroughly enjoying my discomfort at the thought that she might give me away. However, I should have known better, since Ethel loved me too much to ever have embarrassed me in any way. She was just having fun.

Hildegarde gave a small laugh at the story, and said, "I never punched Anna in the nose. But I should have."

For the short while Ethel had left with us on this earth, I was happy to know that I had not only brought her back to life with my stories, but also had given her a chance to be the naughty little girl she always got such a kick out of being.

I was only trying to bring back a semblance of life to people I loved very much, by doing whatever I had to do.

CHAPTER 10

Choices

"I want to go home to die."

And home was Gift of Love.

I had a friend who was one of the early casualties of the AIDS virus. He had been very successful in the fashion world and was fortunate to have the financial resources to decide where and under what conditions he wished to spend his last days. Instead of dying in a hospital environment, hooked up to tubes and trying what was at that time ineffectual treatments for the disease, he chose to stay at home and peacefully listen to his favorite classical music until the end.

Sometimes choice is the only thing left that we can give to a person in the last stages of his or her life. Some measure of control, no matter how trivial it may seem to others, can be immensely important and empowering to someone who has lost everything else. It says to that human being that they are still alive and valuable.

Choices, of course, begin long before the last moments of life. It is an ongoing process that only becomes more precious as someone's independence rapidly starts to decline along with their health.

When the doctor told my aunt Tata that she had a spot on her lung, she knew in an instant that this would be her way out of a life she no longer had any use for.

Instead of possibly prolonging her life with treatment, she was content to go home and wait until she knew it would be too late. She was never morose and we never discussed her choice. When I visited her she was as cheerful as always and had a witty and clever up-to-date take on the happenings in a world she was no longer a part of.

When Tata was at the end of her life, she discovered that the money she thought would take care of her for a lifetime was running out. My mother, who had a great fear of dying in poverty, no matter how rich her husband was, was afraid of spending anything on her own sister, and proceeded to sell all of Tata's jewelry—something that Tata allowed her to do with great grace.

In 1969, one year before she died, I was touring the country as the singer with Guy Lombardo's orchestra, and making something like $300 a week, which was not bad at all in those days.

Each time I received my check, I would send $50 of it to Tata, with a note that said, "I can't give you back your health, but all I can do is share the wealth."

Tata was only seventy-two years old when she died. She was a proud woman who had lived a glamorous and exciting life. At the end she had been reduced to spending her days alone on her couch, with a wheelchair to maneuver whenever it was time for her to go to the bathroom or to bed. She had known the very best of this world and the greatest of tragedies, one having been the loss of her only child. She also had great faith and did not doubt that she would find a peace and comfort in the next world that had often eluded her in this one.

When I saw the look of peace on her face as she lay on her deathbed, I knew that this bright, loving woman had made a wise and courageous choice for herself.

At Gift of Love we took care of numerous nationalities, races, and religions, but there was one delightful Chinese patient who made one day's work unforgettable. He was a young man who came from a family that refused to acknowledge that they had a child with AIDS. For his whole life he had been entirely immersed in the Chinese culture, and although he lived in New York City's Chinatown, he hardly spoke a word of English.

This man's greatest problem at our home was that he had never eaten American food and refused to eat whatever we offered him. We had to believe him when he tried to make us understand that, for him, our kind of food was inedible. He didn't even want to taste it.

Finally the Sisters agreed to a compromise. He would have to write down what he wanted us to go to Chinatown and buy for him to eat, and give us directions on how it should be cooked. We would then make him a sumptuous meal with everything he desired, but after that, he would have to begin to at least *try* our cooking.

He was very precise and most of his meal was not a problem. But when it came to the black chicken, I nearly gagged. It had to be boiled over and over and the water thrown out and replaced several times. And each time the smell of rotten eggs got worse. By the time we were through I wouldn't have touched it for anything in the world.

I can still see him sitting proudly in the dining room with a Chinese banquet in front of him. And he relished every mouthful—even the smelly chicken!

It would have been impossible to do it every day, but we had done everything in our power to make him feel at home. In the end he knew what a special gift it had been for us to honor his culture and his choice of food.

If patients were fortunate enough to regain their strength for a while, there was nothing to prevent their finding an apartment and living an independent lifestyle. We actually encouraged them to leave, so that there would be room for someone who was in crisis and needed a hospice in which to be cared for. The problem with some of our patients' leaving was that they usually went back to their old neighborhoods and old friends who lured them back into the world of drugs—exactly what had landed them in our AIDS hospice in the first place. This was a choice that only they could make and over which we had no control.

It always amazed me that the attraction of drugs could be so strong that some men would give up a safe haven with a bed, meals, medical care, and people to love them, in order to die on the streets smoking crack or with a needle in their arm.

These men were not in the majority, but it was painful to see the self-destructive forces take over the choices some men made at the end of their lives.

A good-looking young Frenchman called Didier had been at our home for some time when he got word from the social worker that his family had sent the airfare for his trip home to France. This was, of course the best of all possible solutions to a bad situation.

On the day of his departure I found one of the nuns packing his suitcase. When she was through she sent him on his way with the words, "Now you go right to the social worker to pick up your ticket and get on the plane today!"

As soon as I heard him hemming and hawing, I thought, "He's not getting on that plane. No way."

One week later, on one of the coldest days of the year, I answered the door and found Didier, dressed in only a flimsy jacket to keep him warm. He had apparently taken the ticket, sold it, gotten high on crack, and in no time had pawned all his belongings, including the suitcase. This young man had been on the streets smoking crack for seven days until there was nothing left.

Sister spoke to him for a while before coming into the kitchen and saying to me, "Tony, why don't you talk to Didier for a while and see what you can do." As soon as I came out of the kitchen she ran down to the convent, leaving me alone with a no-win situation.

When he then told me that his sister was sending him eight hundred dollars to buy another plane ticket, I asked him, "What are you going to do with the money? You're not going to get on that plane, are you?"

"No, I'm not. I'll just get more crack."

"So what do you want from us? What can we do for you?"

"Well, my head isn't right. I'm all confused. . . ."

"How old are you, Didier?"

"Twenty-six."

"The best thing you can do is go home to your family and let them take care of you. If you stay on the street smoking crack, you're not going to live very long."

In the end it was obvious that he didn't really want help for his addiction, and all I could do was give him some warm clothes before he left.

His last words were, "I'll be back."

I never saw him again.

Although it was painful watching Didier walk back down the front steps, his future was in his hands. Leaving the comfort and warmth that we offered him was his choice to make, and there was nothing we could do unless he wanted to help himself.

The predicament for the men who had been addicted to drugs was made clear to me when José, who was doing quite well in spite of chemotherapy for an unusually crippling case of Kaposi's sarcoma on his legs, went to stay overnight at the home of a former resident called Tokio.

When José came back, he told me how much fun it had been to buy food at the grocery store, cook it, watch some television and even have a beer—just ordinary things the rest of us take for granted. His problem lay in the fact that as a former crack addict he immediately recognized the drug dealers in his friend's neighborhood, and as he later told me, "My mind started playing tricks on me."

He said, "That evening, while watching television, I thought, What if I give some money to Tokio and ask him to buy me just a little bit of crack and tell him not to let me do any more? After thinking it over for a while I knew what a fool I was to think it would ever stop there. First it would be a little bit of coke and then I would ask him to go out again. After that I would fight him for the money to buy even more. Before it was over I would rob my friend in order to try and satisfy what would soon become an insatiable need for the drug. I knew there would be no end to it once I started. So I lay there, watched television, and had a nice evening."

He added, "But those are the games an addict's mind plays. You think, '*I* can do that. Sure, I'll just have a little bit.' But it doesn't work that way."

Thank God, José was strong enough and wise enough to make a positive choice at what could have been a dangerous crossroad in his life. Eventually his health improved enough for him to find an apartment with another patient of ours and move out of Gift of Love. I never lost touch with him, and after he died I joined some of his other friends in planning a special funeral service for him in the chapel of St. Clare's Hospital.

Although José did not die at Gift of Love, he knew that because of his positive choices he always had our home to come back to—a home where he knew that he was loved.

At Gift of Love, whether it was a request for a salami sandwich when the patient was in no condition to eat it, or the decision of when to stop using extraordinary measures to prolong a quality of life that no longer existed, I tried to honor the choices the men made.

It is impossible for me to count the times I heard one of our patients who was in the hospital tell the doctors that if there was nothing more the medical community could do for them, then they wanted to come "home" to die. And home was Gift of Love. Sometimes they only had hours left to live, but it was their choice to make, and our duty to honor that choice.

A young man called Augusto made his choice as to where and how he wanted to die, the moment he was brought into Gift of Love. He was very sick when he arrived, and he stayed with us only a few days before having to re-enter the hospital. As the end drew near, he knew there was nothing more the medical profession could do for him and told his doctor, "I want to go back to Gift of Love."

The medical man's reply was, "You know you're only going to live a few more hours. What's the point?"

"I want to go home to die."

As I've said before, the Sisters let the men know that they would greet them with open arms anytime they wanted to come home to die.

When the ambulance workers carried him upstairs, I heard one of them say, "What are we bringing him here for? You know he's going to be dead in no time."

I wish that man had seen the peace on Augusto's face when he died an hour later, surrounded with love. Afterwards we received a beautiful Thank You card from his partner, who stayed with him until the end.

I saw this scenario repeated many times over the years. All of these people were loved enough to be given choices which permitted them to be active participants in the final decisions that would make the end of their lives as meaningful and as peaceful as possible.

CHAPTER 11

Faith

*"God speaks in the silence of the heart,
and we listen."*

—Mother Teresa

"May love bind the book of life for you
And happiness follow its pages through
May the story it tells be of days well spent
And may it close with a clasp of sweet content"

This was a poem that Edward and Agnes Zimmermann wrote on the first page of an autograph book they gave to their daughter Ethel Agnes Zimmerman on June 24, 1920. The book was for her thirty-four classmates to sign their names and write messages of affection and hopes for the future.

Only ten years later, in 1930, the little girl with the autograph book became a sensation on the Broadway stage as the unforgettable star known to the world as Ethel Merman.

Many things have been written about Ethel, some of them by people who never met her or even anyone who *really* knew her. Unfortunately, hatchet jobs are an easy way to make a quick buck, and some folks make a very nice living tearing apart each icon that comes along, attempting to destroy the positive role models we so desperately need in our society today. Even Mother Teresa has had her share of "writers" who made their fortunes putting a scandalous spin on her life.

What impressed me most about Ethel, one of the people closest to me for twenty-five years, was the strong faith that sustained her through many tragedies, including the untimely death of her daughter, whom she adored. It was this kind of faith that allowed her to face her final years, not to mention her own death, *knowing* that she would someday be reunited with her loved ones. Her utter faith in a higher power was one of the little-known facts about this woman whom many thought of as only an extension of her brassy stage roles.

Yes, Ethel had a voice that could shatter glass (or an eardrum that got too close), and yes, she could strut through a performance while she mesmerized the audience into forgetting that there was anyone else in the show, and offstage she could use a four-letter word better than anyone else I ever knew. But she was never dirty. Everything she did was with great humor and taste. The stage persona was something that created a legend which in turn created a fictional Merman that gave performers and writers plenty of material to elaborate on, whether it was true or not.

As for the four-letter words, her detractors have no idea that she did not think it appropriate to use even a "hell" or a "damn" in front of me until I reached the age of twenty-one. But that was her code. And she lived by it.

During all of the years that she carried two Broadway performances on her shoulders (matinee and evening) every Saturday, she never failed to show up at

St. Bartholemew's church with her family bright and early on Sunday morning. She always took communion before the opening night of a new show, and in later years often stopped by during the week just to pray quietly. She never made a show of it, or had to go to church to prove it, but her faith was an important part of her survival and her strength.

The last ten months of Ethel's life, when she lay on her hospital bed at home slowly losing her ability to move or speak, was when she most needed that strong faith to sustain her and give her the grace to face death with a peace that cannot be bought. She had a deep belief in a higher power that would always take care of her and ultimately reunite her with her beloved Mom and Pop Zimmermann and with the daughter she mourned till the end.

Church can be a blessing for many, and an empty, meaningless routine for others. Some may feel pious and above everyone else when they leave a house of worship once a week, but they quickly forget that they should be living their faith every day. Maybe that is why Mother Teresa wanted us to know the joy of giving with our two hands. She was wise enough to understand that whatever you give to others with those two hands will open your heart more than all the sermons you can sit through in a lifetime. At the end of our lives, the real faith in our hearts is the one that will give us the peace we seek.

In the last moments of a peaceful death, we don't think of the grand houses we lived in, the private yachts and jet planes that carried us around the world, or the power, fame, and money we acquired during our lifetime. In every joyful transition that I have seen, the person was only concerned with the love that surrounded them.

Again, a person may have been obsessed with earthly treasures and accomplishments right up until the very end, when in a flash of insight they realize how unimportant those temporary things really are. If there is one loving soul around to gently ease the person towards the light that surrounds them, the life they lived here on this earth will just become part of the lessons they needed to learn before moving on to what I like to call "the best part."

I have often said that fame, money, success, talent, and even great beauty are not gifts but tests. A greater power is watching over us and saying, "Now what are you going to do with it?"

Recently I heard that the last words a famous mogul of the twentieth century said before taking his last breath were, "I'm afraid."

How sad that he only had faith in his business accomplishments and power.

My friend Robert Lehman, the president of Lehman Brothers Banking Investment Corporation and one of the leaders of industry around the world in the last century, was also terrified of dying; and when he had a stroke, he decided that if he never moved a muscle he would preserve all his strength and never die. Sadly, he was quite wrong.

His last year was spent at home, with nurses and

hospital equipment arranged for by his business associates, who at the same time, I am sure, were carefully protecting their own interests.

For a while, a devoted woman who had been one of the caretakers of his estate in Sands Point, Long Island, nursed him lovingly, but she was fired by his associates when they felt that he might be getting too attached to her.

Almost every night of Robert Lehman's final year I had dinner at his apartment with his wife Lee, another of the closest women in my life, and every night I passed by the closed door of the room that had been turned into a mini-hospital for him. Even though he had sometimes been like a father figure to me, I never dared ask if I could enter the inner sanctum of that room.

Lee, who after a suicide attempt the year before had sustained damage to the portion of her brain that controlled her speech and walking, only entered his room once. Her comment to me was, "All Bobbie and I can do is look at each other."

A lifetime of power and the owner of one of the five greatest private art collections in the world had come to this: a frightened man lying in one room of his massive apartment, trying desperately to believe that he would never die.

I wasn't at the apartment when he died, but I hope that he somehow found a peace deep inside to replace the fear. Maybe there was someone there that I don't know about who helped him open the door to a faith that can be granted to us at any time. It's never too late.

Mother Teresa always said, "God speaks in the silence of the heart, and we listen." I pray that he was listening.

At Gift of Love, we were ready to encourage whatever faith the residents believed in. It didn't matter if a nun was saying the "Our Father" or someone else was praying to Allah, it came out the same. They were all talking to the same God.

It surprised me the first time I heard the nuns say to a Catholic patient who was dying, "Give my Love to Jesus and his Mother." And I was equally amazed at the sincerity and fervor with which the patient would invariably say that he would do just that. This kind of faith was sometimes built up over a short time, but at the hour of death had become solid as a rock. How can one not die in peace when they are surrounded by that kind of faith? It was inspiring for me to just be around it.

There were times when I could actually see a beautiful light surrounding the patient, and I would tell them about it. I told them that it was a light from God and that they were protected. Then I would sing "Take My Hand, Precious Lord," and see the peace envelop them like a warm blanket of love.

Our young men often knew just when they were going to die, and when they had faith, it was a joyful transition. They were at peace knowing that they were going "home."

A nurse who worked at St. Clare's Hospital came to visit us at Gift of Love. Before leaving work she had seen

Santos, one of our patients who had gone into the hospital for a procedure. He told her that if she wasn't coming in during the weekend, he wouldn't see her again. He said he was very happy. He was going to heaven.

One of our Sisters said that they had been to see him the day before, and he had also asked them if they would be coming to visit him over the weekend. She answered that they might not be able to come before next Tuesday.

"Oh, Sister," he said, "then I won't see you again because I'll be in heaven next Tuesday." Then he added, "I'm very happy."

The Sisters asked him to say hello to the guys he had known in the house who had passed on before him.

By Tuesday Santos was in heaven.

When a person has lived his or her life controlling not only their own immediate world but also the destiny of others through their power and wealth, they often feel that when they die they will have lost everything of value.

My aunt Mimy, whom I loved very much, once told me that she was frightened of dying and asked me if I could convince her of an afterlife. She hoped that I could give her words of reassurance that her life would go on in some form after death. What she could not understand was how she could exist without the fortune and the castles that gave her life the only meaning she knew.

I was not wise enough at the time to point out that her enormous generosity and the good I knew that she had done for others was all she needed. They would be her passport to a place where the earthly treasures she had always depended upon would no longer be required.

My father was also a skeptic who wanted my reassurance of an afterlife. In some ways I think he *did* believe, but just needed someone like me to confirm his suspicions that life did go on and that, most importantly, he would someday be reunited with my mother.

Sometimes he would try to goad me into giving him tangible proof (something quite impossible for anyone to do) by telling me that he believed in nothing. I would simply answer, "Pop, someday you're in for a big surprise."

When he lay dying in the hospital, I felt the most comforting thought I could give him was that my mother was with him and waiting for him to join her. He could no longer speak, but would lightly squeeze my hand each time I told him she was near.

He had never been a materialistic man or one who cared for power, so I think that, for him, the thought of being reunited with the woman he had loved for fifty years gave him the peace he needed during his final days on earth.

It still amazes me how someone like my father, who had been the kindest and gentlest of men, could ever doubt that a higher power existed, a God who I am sure would gladly embrace a man who had lived such an exemplary life.

. . .

I can well understand the fear of the unknown that surrounds the subject of death, and there are as many ways to deal with it as there are people. Belief that life goes on is something we mere mortals have to accept on faith. Not everyone believes that what is called a "near death experience" is based on fact; many interpret it to be an illusion created by chemical changes in the brain. So there is no concrete evidence to present to anyone who is dying. That is why it is called faith.

I was talking to one of my best friends, Glynnis Snow, about the subject of faith and dying. She told me that she did not need to know what heaven was like. If she *did*, it would be like "opening a package before Christmas."

A few months before Mother Teresa's death, I sat with her on her little terrace in Calcutta and sang for her a song about a person who dreams of going to heaven. This person is greeted by angels and is shown all the wonderful things that await us. When I reached the line where the person says that what they really want is "to see Jesus," Mother Teresa looked into my eyes and nodded her head in agreement.

Mother Teresa was another of the people I knew who needed no reassurance that the God she believed in was ready to accept her into heaven. Her final words on this earth, as she reached up to touch a crown of thorns above her bed, were, "Jesus, I love you. . . . Jesus, I trust . . . Jesus."

Who would not welcome that kind of faith?

CHAPTER 12

Unconditional Love

"The most powerful force in the world."

When my aunt Tata was a young woman, during the Depression, unlike many others, she was living a beautiful, glamorous life. With her inimitable style and wit, she was a part of the famous Round Table at the Algonquin Hotel, with great writers such as Dorothy Parker and Robert Benchley. Elegant nightclubs and accomplished people were a large part of her life.

One night, while leaving a very chic nightclub at 1:00 or 2:00 A.M., she encountered a small nine-year-old boy who, like many others during the Depression, waited until the wee hours of the morning to sell newspapers to the rich and famous as they left the clubs for the journey to their elegant homes.

This little child, who told her his name was Bobby, somehow touched her deeply. She knew that his family desperately needed the few pennies Bobby could earn, and through the years Tata stayed in touch with the little boy as he grew up.

The extraordinary outcome of this story is that Tata eventually put little Bobby through medical school, after which he became a successful doctor with a lovely wife and eight beautiful children, for whom he was able to afford the best education. I am certain that the ripple effect of Tata's unconditional love and generosity ulti-mately changed lives for many generations.

I was very young when I first heard this story, but it resonates more and more in my heart as the years go on and I understand that she was the first one to teach me the real meaning of unconditional love.

While growing up, I always felt that love was conditional. Was I perfect enough to please the grown-ups? Was every hair in place? Were my clothes spotless, my schoolwork beyond reproach? Did I say the right thing, that didn't sound childish?

I could go on and on with my dilemma of needing to be perfect in order to feel worthy of being loved. It was an illusion that I had somehow been conditioned to believe in—a very physically and emotionally exhausting way to go through childhood and beyond. The irony is that I knew from the start how to love others, but did not feel secure in the fact that I could receive it as well.

No doubt my aunt Tata and my maternal grand-mother, Mémé, saw through my obsession with my own perfection, but were powerless to change the patterns of daily life in my home which had created the monster. I do remember Tata trying to build up my confidence by telling me that there was nothing I could possibly do, including murder, that could change her love for me. And Mémé always wrote to me from Boston on my birth-day that I was the most wonderful little boy in the world.

Those were momentary panaceas that, in the long run, were not enough to change my neurotic need to

feel that I really *was* good enough to be loved uncondi-
tionally.

For years I searched for that love and found it in bits
and pieces by attaching myself to "other mothers"—
women who cared for me as though I were their child.
Lee Lehman was the first, when I was thirteen. Then
came Ethel Merman, when I was eighteen. Both relation-
ships lasted a lifetime. But my final healing was from the
little Albanian nun, Mother Teresa.

I had been immediately drawn to this tiny, bent-over
woman and her legion of Missionaries of Charity Sisters
when I first saw that magazine picture of a volunteer in
the Home for the Dying in Calcutta carrying a man in
his arms—a man he had undoubtedly never known
before. This volunteer had been able to love the man
without reservation simply because he was a human
being in need of comfort and care in the last hours of
his life.

That was the legacy Mother Teresa was giving to the
world and I knew immediately that it contained something I had been seeking my whole life. I didn't care
what religion she practiced. I just knew that being
around her would be a giant step in healing the child
within me that had never felt perfect enough to deserve
the love she offered. If I were given the chance to freely
give that kind of love, I knew I would be able to receive
it as well.

I believe it to be the most powerful force in the
world.

* * *

When I think of unconditional love, I think of the many destitute men whom I watched die in Mother Teresa's homes, from New York to Calcutta.

These men came into Gift of Love in New York knowing that they were going to die. These young men, most of them not much more than kids, dealt with a gamut of emotions such as anger, guilt, depression, denial—and sometimes a need to run back into the world for one more desperate fling, to recapture a youth they had either never really had, or felt they were losing all too soon.

Slowly the atmosphere of peace and love created by Mother Teresa and her Sisters helped them to accept the cards they had been dealt in this life. They eventually found that being there for each other as "brothers" helped erase the fear, and replaced it with a sense of purpose in their lives. By helping each other face the pain of this terrible (and at that time, always fatal) disease, they could fill their lives with a sense of usefulness, something many of them had never known before.

Wendell told me on my first day in the house that since coming to Gift of Love he had become particularly attached to I Corinthians 13 in the Bible, which says, "So faith, hope, love abide, these three: but the greatest of these is love."

I don't think he was a devoutly religious person or that he had even read any other part of the Bible. He had just heard that particular verse and liked it.

What I admired most about him was his ability to live what he believed in.

Although his own body had been devastated by AIDS, he would drag himself out of bed to visit any of his friends who were in the hospital. He may have been destitute and living on the Sisters' charity, but he took each of the men a simple gift—sometimes just a piece of fruit, but something he knew that each man liked. Those were real gifts of love.

These men had nothing—no earthly goods and, for the most part, no family. But the moment they started to focus on loving rather than dying they opened themselves up to the possibility of a peaceful death. That kind of generosity is something that can only be born of love.

Donald was a perfect example when one of our most loved volunteers, Peggy Dolan, was leaving for a month in Ireland. As she was saying goodbye, Donald, who had lived on the streets and owned nothing, came running downstairs to the front door with a brand new tee-shirt in his hand, saying, "Darlin', wear this in Ireland. It'll keep you warm with my love."

Even though the men came to us to die, Gift of Love was a house of life and a house of unconditional love.

Although most of our patients went through a difficult time accepting the inevitability of their demise, sooner or later they could not resist the feeling of hope and life that permeated the house.

A little man called Willie was one of the few who

already understood the concept of unconditional love
before he arrived. He did, however, make a unique and
unforgettable entrance into the house.

At 11:30 in the morning one of the Sisters came to
me to say that they were going down to the convent. At
the time I was busy taking care of Wilfredo, who was in
his last days, so the rest of the world in Gift of Love
didn't much matter to me.

I casually asked her, "Who are the other volunteers
right now?"

She answered, "There's only you," and added, "By
the way, all of the Sisters are going out at one o'clock."

At a few minutes to one, the doorbell rang. Standing
at the front door was a little black man of indeterminate
age with two canes.

When he told me he was a new patient named
Willie Jones, I took him up to the dining room so one
of the Sisters could fill out his admittance form. A few
minutes later, on my way to get an ice pack for Wilfredo, Sister stopped me to ask if I would finish Willie's
paperwork since she was in a hurry to leave with the
other nuns.

I wasn't thrilled at leaving Wilfredo alone, and tried
to make the procedure as swift as possible. The main
thing I remember was a list of illnesses that included
AIDS and several kinds of tuberculosis—one of them
being tubercular meningitis.

While Willie sat next to me at the table, his right arm
suddenly went rigid, so I massaged it until the spasm
passed. Then his left leg did the same thing, and he

started answering my questions with, "Buh, buh, buh, buh, buh. . . ."

Although on some level I knew there was a real problem developing, I still had no idea what I was in for. Like a fool, I let the Sisters leave the house, and then said, "All right, Willie, you take it easy for a couple of minutes while I go upstairs and check on Wilfredo."

I felt better about leaving him when he answered, "Uh, okay."

I ran up and down the stairs in record time, but upon my return I found Willie on the floor having a seizure. Not having dealt with a seizure before, I ran down to the kitchen, where another volunteer had just arrived to help prepare dinner. We both rushed back upstairs to the dining room, to find that a patient who had been a medic in the army for four years had taken charge of the situation.

In spite of my panic, I did everything he told me, and paid close attention to the procedure in case it should ever be needed again. Within a few minutes, Willie started to relax and his breathing became normal. Soon he was asleep on the floor. The crisis was over.

As soon as we carried him into the lounge, Willie started to regain consciousness, and the other volunteer was able to go back to his kitchen duties. I then stayed with him until I felt it safe to say, "Now Willie, you know you're going to be all right, so why don't you rest here quietly for a few minutes while I go upstairs and see if Wilfredo needs anything?"

Right away his face filled with panic and he cried,

"No, no, don't leave me. Don't leave me alone. I don't want to be alone. . . . I don't. . . . I don't remember. Where. . . . Where am I?"

Poor little frightened Willie couldn't remember where he was, where he had come from, how he got the clothes he was wearing—nothing—not one thing that had happened to him that day.

I tried to calm him by saying, "You're going to be just fine. You had a little seizure and fainted, but it will all come back to you in a while."

"Oh, oh, I fainted. Oh, my goodness, oh, praise the Lord. Well, where am I now?"

"You're at Gift of Love with Mother Teresa's Missionaries of Charity."

"Oh, oh, then I'm not in the hospital?"

"No, you're not in the hospital. You left the hospital this morning."

"Oh, I don't remember nothing. I don't remember nothing . . . Oh, oh."

"Now Willie, you just relax and take it easy for awhile and it'll all come back to you. You just fainted."

"Oh, I fainted. Oh, my. Oh, praise the Lord."

Again I repeated, "You're here at Gift of Love with Mother Teresa's Missionaries of Charity."

For the first time, he looked around, and said, "This is a nice place. Oh, this is beautiful. Praise the Lord. It's so nice." Then he asked, "And I'm going to stay here?"

"Yes, Willie, you're going to stay here."

"And this is not the hospital?"

"No Willie, this is not the hospital." We went through

this several times until he started to feel his strength returning.

I smiled, "See, I told you you were going to be okay."

By this time I knew I had to get back to Wilfredo upstairs. So when another patient walked into the lounge, I introduced him to Willie and said, "I have to leave you for a few minutes, but as you can see, there are other guys here."

The other man understood immediately and added, "Don't worry, brother. I'll stay here till Tony gets back. I'm with you." It never ceased to amaze me how these men instinctively knew how to take care of each other.

After making sure that Wilfredo was all right, I took Willie upstairs with his few belongings, got him a pair of pajamas, and helped him into bed. He was so grateful for everything.

Willie finally surveyed the room from his bed, and as I put away his things, he exclaimed, "This is such a beautiful place. Oh, praise the Lord. And you're so nice."

He then told me that although he was not a Catholic, he was delighted to see that we had a chapel in the house.

The last thing he said before I went back down the hall to care for Wilfredo was, "Oh, I love Catholics. I love all religions. I love all people. If everybody loved every-body we wouldn't have any problems in this world. I love all religions and all the people in the world!"

He was a great, great man—little Willie Jones with his two canes.

. . .

The end of Willie Jones's life was peaceful and filled with the same unconditional love he so generously shared with us all. It goes to show that everything you give in this world you get back. Thoughts and words are very powerful, and if used in a negative way, have a ricochet effect on the sender. How can someone die in peace if they have lived their life with resentment and hate?

There is also no real unconditional love without humility. If one cannot say "I'm sorry" or accept someone else's sincere apology, they cannot really love or be loved. Unconditional love is not only being able to say you're sorry, but it is also forgiving others for their human frailties. A humble person has no problem with admitting that they don't always do or say the right thing, and understands when someone else errs in *their* judgment.

When Francisco first came to Gift of Love, he was so angry that one night he filled the large fish tank in the lounge with detergent, thereby killing all the fish. The next day Francisco went to the Sisters and confessed to having been the culprit, and offered to clean the tank and replace the fish. When he asked me to lend him the money to buy more fish, I thought that would be the last I would see of those twenty dollars. Within a couple of days, Francisco proved me wrong when he thanked me and paid back the loan.

Francisco's actions transformed a man who had been bitter about his fate into a humble and loving human being. Unconditional love slowly replaced the anger and brought a new respect to this man who was able not only to apologize for his actions but also to make restitution. It was a lesson for each one of us in the house, and brought Francisco closer to a peaceful and loving death surrounded by friends.

Sometimes unconditional love can be a part of our lives, even when it is only an instinctive reaction that could possibly mean the difference between life and death.

Some time in the 1960s I was walking home after an evening at Jim Russo's apartment. It must have been about 1:00 A.M. when I noticed a short man coming in my direction on a very deserted street in New York. When he came closer, he blocked my way, with a large knife in his hand. I stopped in my tracks when he stood in front of me and said, "Give me your money."

I saw the knife, but more importantly, I noticed that his face was covered in perspiration and that he had a deathly pallor.

My first instinct was not about the knife or the threat to my life, but the human suffering I saw before me. I spoke and said in a sympathetic tone of voice, "Oh, you don't look well at all."

The man melted at this unexpected human response, and replied, "You have no idea. In one hour I'm going to be lying in that gutter."

My only thought was not for myself, but for this human being in the midst of a severe drug withdrawal crisis I could only imagine.

I began by asking him what we could do together to help him with his immediate needs and his addiction. I suppose the last thing he had expected that night was a young man with a knife in his face having a sympathetic take on the whole situation.

He put the knife away, while we talked about his options.

Unfortunately, no conclusion was reached, but he was comforted to a certain degree that someone cared about him that night.

Finally, he offered to walk me the few remaining blocks to my home so no one else would accost me. I told him it wasn't necessary, and took five dollars from my wallet and gave it to him. I could only hope he would find the help he needed.

I realized that my unconditional love had quickly eradicated any fear I might have had of this man, and I was able to touch him in a way that would not have been possible had I been fearful and not caring about someone in distress.

As I said before—unconditional love is the most powerful force in the world.

CHAPTER 13

Non-judgment

"I judge no one."

—Mother Teresa

I never tire of quoting Mother Teresa's answer when she was asked what she thought of homosexuality or other controversial subjects that bring out the fear and hatred in otherwise civilized people. She said in her simple, no-nonsense way, "I judge no one."

She was a woman who not only said the words but really lived them every day of her life. She also said, "I love all religions, but I'm *in* love with my own." And even though she did not believe in abortion and believed that each child was conceived to be loved, she didn't just say empty words. Again, she lived them. Mother Teresa was the only religious personage in this world whom I felt had the right to say she did not believe in abortion because she was the only one I heard of who offered to take each child and see that it was raised in a safe and happy environment. As they say, "She put her money where her mouth was!" Even the handicapped babies, many of whom I held in my arms, were happy and assured of a safe place where they could be well cared for with love.

Mother Teresa was a practical woman, but she believed that if her calling was really God's work then He would make all things possible. And He did. Not one baby in over one hundred countries in the world was ever turned away from her orphanages. There was always room for one more child.

From her homes in New York City to those in Calcutta, I saw firsthand the attitude of non-judgment that Mother Teresa instilled in her Missionaries of Charity Sisters. Everyone's religious belief was honored, and at the end of their lives the men and women who died in her homes were buried or cremated accordingly. In Calcutta, whenever a man who was unconscious was brought to the Home for the Dying and died without regaining consciousness, his religion was sometimes ascertained by whether he had been circumcised or not. Everyone was respected.

At Gift of Love we received a whole range of young men with different lifestyles. I once heard the Sisters roar with laughter when a gay patient jokingly said he did not want to receive the sacraments of the church from a particular priest because the man was not "cute enough!" The Sisters had a good enough sense of humor to know they were being teased, and laughed along with the rest of us.

As for the prisoners who were paroled to us to die, it never occurred to me to ask what their crime had been. It didn't matter anymore. The world of drugs the majority had probably been involved in, and which had ultimately caused their illness, was of no importance. They knew they were dying, and our job was to give these young men a beautiful death, not to focus on the painful lives they had often been forced to live.

When Ricardo was in the last stages of AIDS, Sister

tried to tell me about a person who came to visit him. She used the word "friend" and made it sound as though it were in quotes. This was not said in a judgmental way, but rather as a preparation for any encounter I might have with this friend.

That evening, when Ricardo's friend arrived, my first impression from the top of the banisters was that it was a woman. But when I heard a very deep voice chatting with the nuns, I realized it was a man dressed in a very sexually ambiguous manner.

Having never seen the Sisters in this kind of situation before, I was curious as to how they would react. Although they may live their lives taking care of all kinds of human beings, most of the nuns, I believe, come from rather unsophisticated backgrounds.

Within moments I knew that I needn't have worried. They were as thrilled as I was to see a loved one come into the house, and felt no reason to judge the way this person dressed or spoke. The only thing that mattered was that a friend or relative was there to comfort a patient and make them feel a connection of love. And if that patient was very sick, the visitor was more than welcome to stay all day.

I suppose that kind of non-judgment is born of humility. Mother Teresa never thought of herself as anyone special. As she once wrote to me, she was a pencil in God's hands. "He does the thinking—He does the writing—everything."

. . .

One could easily have condemned the young men who came to Gift of Love after they got AIDS from sharing infected needles with other addicts. But all our circumstances in life are different. We are born to different families in different parts of the globe. We have different socio-economic situations to deal with and different strengths and weaknesses that shape our lives.

The whole concept of respecting someone's lifestyle and religious beliefs makes it possible for that person to die in peace.

In the end we have to answer to God and not each other.

No one on this earth is given a free ride. We are all given our own burdens to cope with. And those who think that having great wealth or talent gives one immunity to pain and suffering are quite misguided, and usually do so out of a sense of envy. If we could walk in each other's shoes for one minute we would find, in short order, that we far preferred our own baggage to anyone else's. After all, our own baggage is what we are here to take care of as best we can, so it's the baggage we are most comfortable with.

But if at the end of someone's life we can help them reach a part of the divinity that lies within each of us, they will be able to look forward to the passage into the next stage of their existence. They will know that their body may become dust but their soul will live on.

. . .

As far as I can see, humility and non-judgment go hand in hand. Every man or woman whom I have watched die has left with a look of peace on their face and a joyful expectation of whatever they believed awaited them. This would not have been possible if they had been made to feel that they were being looked down upon and judged instead of being loved just the way they were.

As Mother Teresa said, "We have all been created to love and be loved."

CHAPTER 14

Signs from Beyond

"All we have to do is ask."

The older I get, the more I understand that we are divinely prepared for our tasks in this life. If God wanted me to ease anyone's final moments on this earth, I needed many lessons before I could have an inkling of how to begin. These were lessons I felt compelled to learn.

A few days before my aunt Tata died, my parents went to visit her in the hospital. None of us had talked about it, but we all knew that her death was imminent. As soon as they arrived, Tata turned to my mother and announced with great joy that their mother had been to visit her earlier that day.

My mother, who was known for her practical side, wasted no time telling Tata that it was impossible since their mother had been dead for twenty-four years. After Mother left the hospital, poor Tata was embarrassed that her sister might think that she had been hallucinating.

It took me years to understand that Tata had indeed had a valid visit from her mother, who came to help her through the transition we call death.

It seems that as we come closer to the end of our lives on this earth plane, a visit from a loved one who has already passed over is not an unusual occurrence. I believe that they come to reassure us that life *does* go on, and that we do not make the journey alone.

It is undeniable that many dying people "see" and talk to someone at their bedside—someone they have loved and trusted who has gone on before and is now there to help them find their way at the end. I have seen it too many times to doubt it. Often a look of euphoria comes over the dying person's face as they call out the name of someone only they are meant to see.

I cannot count how many times and in how many forms this scenario has been played out before me, not only among my family and friends but also at Mother Teresa's homes for the dying.

Wilfredo, in his last days at Gift of Love, kept talking about a beautiful woman who had appeared to him. He was filled with joy as he tried to put into words the radiance that surrounded her. Of course, the Catholic nuns interpreted it as having been a visitation from the Virgin Mary. I, on the other hand, was open to the possibility of its being any spirit who was watching over him— maybe even a grandmother or a great-aunt who had died before he ever met her. All that mattered to me was that a loving presence had come to ease his passing and give him proof that life is eternal.

Many children are born with the ability to see things from one dimension to another. In their innocence, they talk about the spirits that only they can see. These are what parents often refer to as their child's "imaginary playmates."

More often than not the children are made to feel uncomfortable and are scolded for "talking nonsense." Eventually most of them reach an age where the knowledge and ability to see beyond this earthly dimension disappears, while others, in spite of the public pressure to deny what they see, are able to grow up with their gift intact. Many of them ultimately use these abilities to enlighten and comfort others.

On the other hand, we must watch out for the charlatans who prey on the gullible and make them believe that they, the scam artists, are endowed with psychic and healing gifts which they do not have. The only talent these folks have is to bilk grieving family members out of money they can often ill afford to lose. Grief can sometimes make intelligent men and women trust the most heinous of criminals.

In the final analysis, I believe that we can all sit quietly and in our meditation feel the very real presence of our loved ones, without anybody else's intervention.

It's no surprise to me that at the beginning and end of life we are often able to see what lies on the other side of the "invisible" curtain that separates us from the mysteries of the universe.

And why do most of us lose that ability as we grow up?

Probably because it would interfere with the purpose we came into this life to accomplish. What good would it do if we had too much knowledge? How would we learn if we could not make mistakes along the way?

If we had all the answers there would be no reason to be here in the first place.

I have never understood, however, the purpose of someone like me, who has sporadic experiences with the "other side"—experiences over which I have little control. I know there has to be a reason for everything, but sometimes that reason is not clear to my all too human brain.

At about the age of five I had an experience so profound that I never could discern if it happened in a dream state or not. The physical and emotional aspects were more powerful than anything I had ever known, and today the memory is as clear as it was all those years ago.

The first thing I remember was being brought by a loving spirit through a field of beautiful flowers with rabbits and other small animals running about. The colors were more vivid than any I had ever seen before, and each living thing radiated a feeling of joy. The whole garden was infinite in its grandeur and welcomed me with nothing but comfort and love. I did not know where I was, but I had no fear and felt completely at home. In an instant I knew that this was a place I never wanted to leave.

In the midst of the intense beauty, I saw a small welcoming chalet with an older couple standing in the doorway waiting to greet me. As I walked through the field towards the house, I stopped from time to time to touch the friendly animals that crossed my path.

Although I was taking my time and enjoying the garden, I knew the couple had been expecting me. The
moment I reached the doorstep they wrapped their
arms around me and showered me with a warmth and
affection I could not have imagined on an earthly level.
I knew I was home, and for the short time I was allowed
to visit, I wanted nothing more than to stay forever in
this atmosphere of unconditional love and bliss.

It was the loveliest experience of my young life and
one I will never forget. I don't know why I was given this
gift—maybe it was to give me courage for the trials of
sexual abuse and fear I would soon have to face as a
youngster. Or maybe by showing me another dimension
that we ultimately come back to, it would prepare me for
my work with the dying many years later. All I know is
that I am grateful for the experience, and if this was a
glimpse of what heaven is like, we all have something
beyond our earthly imaginations to look forward to.

That was the first childhood experience I can remember
that dealt with other dimensions, and although it was
the most comforting, it was not the last.

At the age of seven I occasionally felt the need to
dress up as an old immigrant lady with a babushka and
a grey woolen shawl around my shoulders. Everyone in
the house would then gather in the living room while I
related the story of my life. It was most amusing to the
rest of the household, but did not feel like a game to me.
The tragedies that emerged, especially those of my many
children who each had a name and a story, were very

real to me. My heart would break every time I sat in that chair trying to come to terms with the pain I had endured in that lifetime.

Today most of the stories elude me, but I can still remember the sadness and compulsion to make someone understand how difficult what I believe was a past life had been. I may have been poorly dressed and owned nothing, but I had a dignity that drew everyone in the house to listen to—as she called herself—Madame Go.

That was the beginning of my belief that we are reborn many times, until we have purified our souls by learning the lessons that can only be taught by living on this earth and inhabiting these fragile bodies. No one can say that hatred and the greed for money and power that rules this world makes it a Utopia. It is a learning ground and not what I call heaven.

Whenever I say to Jim Russo, my partner of fifty years, that I *know* something, he can tell by the way I say the word *know* that it is information from a psychic place. It doesn't happen often, and sometimes he tries to question me on subjects he is curious about, but I'm not sure that I can—or want to—make it work at will. More often than not it catches me by surprise. However, I never doubt its validity.

When I was a child at my grandmother's château in France, I looked at my step-uncle, who was a young man engaged to be married, and suddenly *knew* that he would never have a child—something I believe would have been very dear to him. And he never did. A year later his wife miscarried and was never pregnant again.

As time went on, I did not believe that all the information that came through was of a particularly useful nature. Therefore, as an adult I learned how to "turn off" any intuitive thoughts that made me uncomfortable.

In the early 1980s I discovered that several times a day I would say the word "poor," followed by the name of someone I knew. The phrase just popped out of my mouth unwillingly and the name was always the same until about six months later, when that person would die. At a later date it would begin again with someone else's name. When it dawned on me that the outcome was always the same and that there did not seem to be a helpful purpose to the information, I consciously shut it down. Now, whenever the dreaded words try to pop out, I deny them and ask for it not to happen again. So far I have been successful.

Ethel Merman had a similar but more immediate gift. She had no idea that she was psychic until I told her. She must have trusted my judgment, because after that she went around telling friends, "I'm psychic, you know!"

She also had a great healing energy with those who were ill. I could see people find a new strength and comfort entering their bodies and minds while she sat by their bedside, gently talking to them and holding their hand.

Ethel had one gift, however, that made me uneasy. Whenever we came home from a party and she would say, "So and so doesn't look well at all," that person would invariably be dead within a week. I finally asked her never to tell me if I didn't look well. I didn't want to take any chances!

She was absolutely correct in one last prediction about someone's death—her own. Although both her parents lived into their nineties and she had always enjoyed unusual good health and stamina, she always said that she would die in her seventies. She left us at the age of seventy-six.

The only times I can honestly say that I have welcomed my own intuition was when I could see a positive purpose in the experience.

The last time Jim Russo and I drove away from his mother's house and saw her wave goodbye from her front door, I *knew* that we would never see her again. At the time, we were scheduled to leave the States and go back to France to work. Soon after, we were in Paris when I got the phone call that Anna Russo, who had seemed in perfect health, had died peacefully while taking an afternoon nap.

The next day we flew back to New Jersey for the funeral.

It was an emotional time for everyone as we lined up outside the funeral home to view the body. I remember Jim's sister, Louise, who was visibly grief-stricken, asking Jim if she could hold onto his arm. I walked in directly behind them and found it particularly painful to watch two people I loved go through the agony of seeing their mother's dead body for the first time.

My own emotions were on shaky ground, but as I came within several feet of the coffin I felt a wave of extraordinary peace wash through my body—a peace that only intensified as I came closer.

At first I was certain that everyone else could feel the same thing I did. It was so powerful that I even "played" with it for a while. I would back up and feel the intensity of the feeling recede and then return in full force as I came closer to the casket. It was as though a halo of peace had enveloped the whole area surrounding their mother.

To this day I wonder. Was it her? Or was it spirits who had come to comfort the mourners? These are questions I have never been able to answer. I only know that it was a real and very powerful experience.

Later, I was surprised to find out that I was the only person who had experienced the loving peace emanating from the area around the body.

That feeling of someone I can't see wrapping my whole being in a cocoon of love has happened at other times in my life, but never under those same conditions. However, after Anna Russo's funeral I couldn't help but wonder why I had not been comforted in a similar fashion fourteen years earlier when my own mother passed over. Instead, I was given a different but not so comforting experience.

A few nights after Mother died, I had a vivid dream. It was one of those dreams where each of your senses is heightened and you *know* you have reached another realm in that subconscious state.

In the dream I saw my mother in her pale blue peignoir, looking as beautiful as ever, standing in an empty place. She looked composed but not joyful. I felt she was still attached to the earth plane and had not yet found her way.

I was overjoyed, and ran to where she was standing alone. I then put my arms around her and kissed her. The feel of her skin, the smell of her perfume, and the touch of her hair near my face were all as real as when I had come home every day from school, years before, and embraced her on her chaise longue in the pink bedroom she and my father shared.

The only words I thought to say to her as I savored that very real moment was, "Mother, can you help us?"

She looked far away into the distance and answered with a touch of sadness in her voice, "But darling, I died."

That was the last time I saw my mother. On many occasions since then I have felt her loving presence nearby, but I have never *seen* her again.

As I get older and more open to my beliefs that there is no "death" and that life goes on, I can accept the thin line that separates us from those we love and ask them for guidance and support.

At first I felt strange asking Mother Teresa for help. I thought that she would be too busy taking care of much needier cases than mine. Then I felt a definite response throughout my body each time I thought about her, and realized I was looking at it from an earthly standpoint. She would never abandon me, any more than my mother and father or Tata would. The cord of love is always there and unbreakable.

All we have to do is ask.

Several years ago, I read a spiritual book about the mysteries of the universe and how we are all connected. It was a difficult book for me to follow, since I would invariably fall into a deep sleep after reading only a few pages. To tell the truth, my eyelids would begin to grow heavy after the first couple of lines. It was particularly hard to make sense out of the words while trying to stay awake.

Even though I had a hard time staying awake for more than a few minutes after picking up the book, I was always anxious to pick it up again. Eventually, I made it through to the end.

The night that I finished the book, I began to have a series of "dreams," the kind that are too vivid not to be inspired by a wiser and more spiritual source than ourselves. These dreams continued for a period of six months and did not occur every night. If they had, I would have been too exhausted to function in the daytime.

In these dreams I was taken to different realms that exist not only on our earthly sphere but in other dimensions of the universe as well. Each time was a totally different experience with a new lesson for me to learn.

I understood from the start that I was only given as much as my tiny human brain could absorb. Whatever spiritual intelligence was guiding me let me know the magnitude of the reality of what I was shown without "blowing all my fuses."

Many of the dreams have now retreated into my subconscious and I trust will surface at the appropriate time. But many have stayed in my mind with the same clarity as when I awakened from them.

One night I was shown the essence of unconditional love. Another night it was the pain that we create on this earth. Again I was aware that these subjects were too enormous for me to completely take in, and I understood that my experience was a taste of something much larger than one human being could experience. However, the taste was sufficient for me to understand the importance of the subject.

At other times I traveled to other dimensions that I remembered having visited between other lives. One such place gave me the impression of a barren planet. There were no other people around and all was in varying tones of grey. The only tangible thing I perceived was a round rock large enough for me to sit on. In spite of the seemingly cold aspect of this place, I felt a great peace and serenity that had been necessary for me after a turbulent lifetime. It was a place where my spirit could be enveloped and restored in the kind of healing balm that I required at that time. I also knew that I would move on when the time was right.

Throughout the whole experience in that place, I had no doubt that a loving presence I like to call God was watching over me, and that the reality of life after death may be much broader than our traditional human concepts. After all, why shouldn't a higher and wiser power have a few (or many) surprises for us that our little human minds cannot conceive of?

At the end of six months I had what turned out to be the last, and the most memorable, dream of the series—one that taught me more about myself than I had ever learned in all my years on this earth.

This time I found myself in what felt and looked like a dark, subterranean cave with high ceilings. Although this could have been an intimidating atmosphere, I had no fear. Before long, a beautiful man dressed in magnificent robes walked toward me. At first I couldn't help but be impressed by the sheer physical beauty of this being as he approached me with a warm smile on his face. But as soon as he came close I became aware of the unspeakable evil that was masked by the physical beauty.

Before he could touch me I repudiated him and told him that I wanted no part of the evil I saw standing before me. As soon as the words were out of my mouth I watched this creature melt into a grotesque manifestation of the satanic being that I had sensed. Then, one after the other, I was presented with more men and women trying to seduce my soul with their beauty. I repudiated them all as evil, and as I did so, each one in turn was transformed into the hideous physicality that represented their true souls. Not only could my eyes see the horror they represented, but I could feel the rage that my rejection brought out in them.

Their fury and frustration only gained momentum when I fell on my knees and started to pray. I had no fear. I knew I was divinely protected. Again, all I had to do was ask.

When they understood that they were losing the battle, the monsters surrounded me and tried to beat and overpower me with crude sticks and vile curses. But they could not reach me. I was enclosed in an invisible, protective shell that contained a power much stronger than theirs.

I felt a strange exhilaration when I awakened from this dream. It was as though I had been presented with a final exam in school and had passed the course. Not only that, but I felt an invisible hand patting me on the shoulder and saying, "Well done!" The hand stayed on my shoulder for three days.

I never had another of those "dreams" again.

An end to this life as we know it is a road we will all take sooner or later. But we can be assured that with enough love and compassion, we *can* help our loved ones in their last days on this earthly plane, and that the human spirit can never be destroyed.

CHAPTER 15

The Real Saints

*"Everything you give to God,
you get back."*

When one hears the word "saint," one naturally thinks of the obvious, such as Mother Teresa. But if we look around us, we will find that throughout our lifetime we are surrounded by saints. The only difference between them and Mother Teresa is that they are not known to the world. The irony of it is that Mother never sought out fame. Actually she shunned it until it hunted her down and became a part of her destiny in creating a "bridge of love around the world."

One of the miracles of her work is that it was done without accepting church or state funding. Had she allowed it, they would have had the power to tarnish her work by making her beholden to them. She believed that if it was God's work, the money would appear by "divine providence." She opened hundreds of homes for the poor in more than one hundred countries, just with donations from everyday people.

In any case, although money was necessary, it was secondary to the fact that she really wanted you and me to learn the joy of giving with our own two hands by joining her and her Missionaries of Charity Sisters and Brothers in the work.

Before meeting her, I never thought of how the

world at large responded to the presence of a woman considered to be a living saint. The first time I was with her in a public setting outside of her convents was in a large cathedral where a group of her nuns were being professed.

At the start of the mass there was a long procession, which wound around the church. This included dozens of the church hierarchy, wearing golden robes, and full of all the pomp and ceremony they could muster for the occasion. Every seat was taken and all eyes remained solemnly on the door from which they were entering.

At the tail end, a tiny, elderly nun walked in, with her head bowed low and her weathered hands in a position of prayer. Mother Teresa had arrived, in her neatly mended simple blue and white sari. It did not matter how gloriously the priests and cardinals were adorned, this was what the congregation had been waiting for.

I wish I could say that the crowd kept a respectful demeanor, but I was shocked at the way these supposedly civilized people behaved when she came into view. They not only ran into the aisles to flash their cameras inches from her face, but they felt compelled to touch every accessible part of her body as she walked by. It was as though they expected to find the key to heaven by physical contact with her, creating a kind of frenzy I found inappropriate and more than a little frightening.

On the other hand, *her* demeanor never changed. She continued walking to her place in the first row of the church with her head still bowed and her hands still clasped in prayer. She seemed so completely in communion with God as to be oblivious to her surroundings.

Whenever possible, and in spite of her failing health, she would often stand at the back of the church after a service and greet each person—whether there were a hundred people or a thousand. Each one was blessed by Mother and given a miraculous medal that she blessed and kissed. She sometimes stood for hours while the faithful filed by, falling on their knees and weeping at her feet. She treated each individual with as much love and reverence as she had had for the man she had picked up from the gutters of Calcutta and brought home to die "like a king."

There were many "saints" I encountered during my years with Mother Teresa and her Missionaries of Charity. They didn't have to pray all day or even pray at all. They just had to be there when there was a need. What they *did* was the real prayer.

One evening during my first month at Gift of Love, I ran downstairs to answer the doorbell and found a well-dressed young man called Michael standing on the steps. He said he was a volunteer with an AIDS project from St. Francis of Assisi and that he had visited one of our patients, Wendell, at Bellevue Hospital. When the hospital told him that Wendell had gone AWOL, he remembered their having talked about Gift of Love and decided to come and see how he was doing.

I knew that some of the staff on the AIDS floor at Bellevue were so frightened of the disease that unless the patients had family or friends to help them, their meals were sometimes left on a table far away from their reach. Many times, while visiting one of our men, I had to go over and help a dying man eat a few mouthfuls of his supper before someone came and whisked his tray away.

On his way out, after visiting Wendell, Michael told me that he was a businessman who worked full time and afterwards visited AIDS patients. He would sometimes bring a flower for a dying man to smell or look at, or he would ask them if they wanted to say a prayer with him. It didn't matter what he did, it only mattered that he was there and that they were not alone for a little while. I will never forget his final words to me that day as he went out the door, "There's such a need, and *I have no choice.*"

In the early days of AIDS, prisons as well as hospitals had no idea how to cope with the disease. The staff was not only helpless to give medical care, but they were also understandably frightened because no one knew how AIDS was transmitted. For these reasons they were only too happy to parole dying inmates into our care.

A patient called José was brought to us by his parole officer. On the way to Gift of Love, José told him that the one thing he wanted more than anything else in the world was a pizza. So the officer stopped off and bought José a pizza. He later told me how gratifying it had been to be able to give this simple but immense pleasure to a man who has just spent a couple of years in jail and was coming to Gift of Love to die.

This parole officer had to deal with many dying inmates, and his way to avoid burnout was to take advantage of the seemingly little contributions he could make—little things like a piece of pizza for men like José, and then visiting them in the hospital or at Gift of Love. After they passed on, he would show his respect by going to the funeral or memorial service, thereby lending some dignity to that person's life. By doing those small things, he made his job worthwhile and uplifting to his spirit.

I don't even know this parole officer's name, but I think of him as one of those saints who touched many dying people's lives with small gestures which held the greatest power of all—the power of love.

Taking one of our men to any emergency room in the city, especially at St. Clare's Hospital, was often a daylong wait to see a doctor. On the other hand, St. Clare's seemed to be one of the most willing to try and cope with the limited medical options available for AIDS patients.

One morning I arrived with Ricardo, who was in a great deal of pain and had a high fever. That day I was told that there was only one doctor on duty for a twelve-hour shift.

After a couple of hours I requested a gurney for Ricardo to lie on. Periodically I asked him, "How are you doing?" and he would bravely answer, "I'm fine." A little while later, when he couldn't stand it anymore, he would sit up on the stretcher, put his head in his hands, and cry, "Oh, I hurt very much." All I could do was stroke his back and let him know that he was not alone.

For most of the day, in spite of his suffering, his greatest concern was for *me.* He kept asking whether I was hungry, whether I was tired, or if I wanted to sit down. And every time I did anything for him he would thank me profusely. I couldn't get over the fact that during the seven hours we waited to see the doctor, *my* comfort was always on this dying man's mind.

Surely there must be a heaven for that kind of generosity.

Another inspiring highlight of that long day at St. Clare's Hospital was when a large, middle-aged Hispanic woman walked through the Emergency Room right after we arrived, saw us sitting there, called out, "Ricardo!" and threw her arms around him.

This simple, motherly figure had lost her twenty-four-year-old son to AIDS the year before, and had volunteered at the hospital ever since. She made it her job to go around the hospital kissing and hugging the AIDS patients, regardless of the lesions covering their bodies and faces, and gave unconditional love to each one. She spent her days comforting many young men who in the last days of their lives became her "sons." And she became "Mama" to them all.

Before she left us, she turned to me and said, "What you do is beautiful. Everything you give to God, you get back."

The tragedy of her loss was the impetus for her to

help countless other young men like her son and at the same time help heal some of her own pain.

I will never forget her.

It was also gratifying to see the way the merchants in the neighborhood so generously supported our hospice. A caterer came to our door one day with a crate of extra food. As a result, everyone had tortellini for dinner. There was even enough left over for us to send to the soup kitchen in the Bronx. Sometimes the bakery sent over beautiful pastries, and when they would see the Sisters walk by, they would run out and fill their arms with freshly baked bread.

I never minded the extra steps to answer the doorbell, because it was so often a testimony to people's generosity. And everything was used—nothing was ever wasted.

Peggy Dolan, one of our most loved volunteers and another person I consider a saint, heard that it was the feast day of one of the Sisters who had been born and raised in Italy. She went to an Italian bakery and said she wanted an assortment of sweets so the Sisters could celebrate. When she mentioned it was for Mother Teresa's Missionaries of Charity, the owner came out and said that she would personally take care of everything. The woman then put together a beautiful box of Italian pastries for which she refused any payment. The Sisters were delighted when Peggy brought them to the convent. Peggy knew, however, that the nuns might have a small taste, but would invariably give most of them to the poor—an act that would give them more joy than all the pastries in the world.

There were many fine doctors and nurses that I came in contact with during my twelve years at Gift of Love. But I was witness to some whose dedication surpassed my greatest expectations.

The first one who comes to mind is Stephen, a nurse who stayed with me the whole day I spent with James in the clinic waiting for a room to become available. There was little that could be done for someone who was locked in his own body, unable to take care of himself, communicate, or see, but the doctor wanted to at least *try* to ease his suffering.

From the moment we arrived, James fought off anyone who attempted to take his temperature or blood pressure. When the time came to move him to a room, we had to wait a couple of hours before James was calm enough for us to untie him from the wheelchair and put him in the bed. We had been afraid that he might throw himself out of the chair and hurt himself.

Finally, after James's resistance began to wear down, the doctor was able to give him a shot of Haldol. It had taken several hours to get to this point, but when I saw James smile at me through the haze of drugs, I knew I could finally go home. I no longer cared if it was an artificial calm from the storm. Whatever gave him even temporary comfort at the time was okay with me.

And the nurse, Stephen, never left James's side. He

did everything in his power to comfort James in his distress, and to let me know that I was not alone to cope with the situation.

The next day I dropped off a little gold guardian angel pin for him at the hospital. Another volunteer had given it to me at Gift of Love, but I thought Stephen had really earned it the day before for service beyond the call of duty.

It's funny how you know when someone *really* cares, and I'm sure that the patient can feel it also.

Another nurse whom I will always remember also worked at St. Clare's Hospital. I only met her briefly the day I was bringing Wilfredo in for his last trip to the hospital before he came back home to us to die. But I could tell right away how much she cared about each of her patients on the AIDS floor.

It wasn't anything she particularly said or did that impressed me, it was her whole demeanor—a demeanor that exuded unconditional love. I knew right away that my friend Wilfredo could not be in better hands.

I was also certain—and I will put my hand in the fire on this one—that she was a transsexual. She looked and sounded like Ernest Borgnine in drag. But I fell instantly in love with a great human being. There was no doubt that Wilfredo would be well cared for by someone who was totally dedicated to her calling, and it was safe for me to leave.

It still makes me smile when I think how fortunate I

was to meet people who could share that much love with the world, and make a difference in the lives of terminally ill patients.

And they would probably tell you that they were just doing their job.

CHAPTER 16

Never Forgotten

"I'm HO-OME, I'M HO-OME!"

—Max, at the gates of Heaven

As I wrote in my memoir, *Ethel Merman, Mother Teresa . . . and Me,* during the twelve years I volunteered at Gift of Love, helping more than one hundred men who died of AIDS, most of the patients were young enough to have been my sons. Indeed, I thought of them as "my kids." Unfortunately, in those days, AIDS was a death sentence, and all of "my kids" died within a few months. Some of their stories, below, illustrate why Gift of Love was a place of life, not of death.

ROBERTO

One of the first of "my kids" to die at Gift of Love was Roberto, a small young Hispanic man who had a club foot. In an attempt to keep from losing his sight, he spent eight hours a day hooked up to an IV stand that looked bigger than he did. In spite of that, Roberto never stopped running up and down the stairs, smiling at everyone. How could anyone not love a kid with that kind of spirit?

Towards the end, Roberto finally lost the fight to save his eyesight and could see only shadows. When the priest came to visit him, Roberto asked, "Father Tom, will you speak at my funeral?"

"Sure, Roberto. What do you want me to say?"

Roberto, with an impish grin on his face, answered, "I want you to say what a wonderful guy I was!"

I could only wonder where this kind of courage came from.

GILBERT

Gilbert was the healthy-looking, muscular young patient who opened the front door for me the first time I entered Gift of Love as a prospective volunteer, when I went for my interview with Sister Maria Lucy, who was then the Superior in charge of the house. Gilbert had been a drug addict who had grown up surrounded by poverty, but was now giving lectures at drug rehabilitation centers—using his own life and battle with AIDS as an example of the dangers of drugs.

The first time I went into his room he proudly showed me boxes of flowers growing on his windowsill. He called them his "babies" and told me that when one was particularly beautiful he would put it in the chapel in front of a statue of the Virgin Mary.

On Gilbert's thirtieth birthday, the Sisters announced that we were going to have a party for him and asked me to help. Then, for the first time in my life, I decorated a cake. I covered it with chocolate icing, added sugar flowers, and wrote "Happy Birthday Gilbert" on it. That night I stayed through dinner so I could carry the cake into the dining room and sing "Happy Birthday" with the men.

After blowing out his candles, Gilbert told me that this had been the best birthday of his life.

That just about took my breath away.

JAMES

It was never easy to get James to the clinic for his periodic evaluation. He would panic the minute he knew he had to leave the safe environment of Gift of Love.

The last time I told him I was taking him to St. Claire's Hospital, he refused to eat his breakfast or take his pills. He kept repeating the one word that came easily to him in his frustration and fear, "NO! NO! NO!," and for the first time I saw him cry.

Two hours after we arrived at the hospital, the doctor was ready to see James. By then James was crying again and it took three of us to maneuver him into the office. Between sobs, he managed to repeat over and over, "Help me! Help me!"

Dr. Jones wiped the tears from James's face and said, "Yes, James, we're going to help you. We're going to help you." He then turned to me and asked, "Do you know what a locked-in syndrome is?"

Although I said "No," I could have guessed what he was going to say, since I had already been through it with Ethel Merman during her last days.

"It's when you're fully conscious but since part of your brain has been damaged, you can no longer communicate or make your body do what you want it to. In essence you're locked in—imprisoned within your own body." Then he added, "I've got to admit him. We have to do a complete workup and see how we can help this man."

Later, in the hallway, Dr. Jones said to me, "Another minute and I would have burst out crying."

Back in the waiting room, the other patients, mostly convicts from a New York prison, also tried to calm James. But James was locked in his own nightmare.

Five hours after we had arrived, James's room was ready. When we took him to his room, he was still hysterical, crying and sobbing, "No! No! No!," but exhaustion was beginning to set in.

Finally the nurse and I decided to try to put him on the bed. He was lying quietly on his side when a doctor— with his hair in a ponytail, and wearing a tee-shirt with a comic strip character printed on it—came in to give him a tranquilizer, take his temperature and blood pressure, set up an IV, and draw several vials of blood.

It had been a long day and I was so drained that I watched the blood spurt out of James's arm and thought, "I've never been able to watch a needle even go into an *orange* in my life, and this act means no more to me than the Looney Tunes cartoon on the doctor's shirt." After all the suffering I had seen that day, this flesh and blood act meant nothing. It wasn't scary. It wasn't anything.

At five o'clock I went over to a now-smiling James and said goodbye. Although his good humor was drug induced, just seeing him look happy made me feel better.

Back at the house, I went into the lounge where the

men were. I didn't want to depress them so I only told them that James was smiling when I left the hospital. But I suspected that they could see the disturbing effects of the day on my face.

I then stayed with the men, who were of varying religions, while they sat together and prayed for the Sisters, the volunteers, each other, their families and their friends in the hospital.

When I got up to go home, Gilbert came over, put his hand on my shoulder, and asked how I was doing. Then Wendell, who had had to ask for nausea medication during the prayers, said, "Will you give me a hug?" Each of the men in the room came up to me and put his hand on my shoulder or had a comforting word for me.

I couldn't believe it. These guys dying of AIDS were giving so much more to me than I could ever give back.

SCOTT

When Scott, at the age of fifteen, told his parents he was gay, they immediately disowned him, announced that he was no longer their son, and threw him out of the house. He was a handsome young man who, like so many others, was then forced to do many things in order to survive on the streets.

He was eighteen years old when a doctor told him he was HIV-positive. In desperation he turned to his family for support, but they told him it was God's judgment for his sexuality, and he could only come home if he changed his "aberrant lifestyle."

One day as we sat alone in the dining room, he blurted out, "Tony, do you know what I want to be when I grow up?"

"No, Scott, what do you want to be when you grow up?"

"I want to be Patsy."

I was stymied for a moment until a light bulb went off in my head, and I asked, "You mean Patsy Stone from the British television series *Absolutely Fabulous?*"

"Yeah, that's what I want to be when I grow up."

At first I thought he was just being funny. Then I understood that Patsy Stone was a glamorous character who could go to any lengths with her outrageous or incorrect behavior and remain totally invincible. The "piper" never got paid and she always survived—very seductive stuff for a kid who was dying of AIDS.

MAX

Since all of Mother Teresa's homes were created for the poorest of the poor, social workers sent us as many homeless cases as we could handle. At Gift of Love I discovered that they were simply human beings in need— human beings with whom I could build a relationship of respect and caring.

Before Max moved into the house he had lived in homeless shelters for years. Gift of Love was the first home he had known in a long time. He told me that he had earned his living by traveling from one end of the city to the other every day, pushing a supermarket cart which he filled with recyclable cans. I could tell how much he had loved his work and, although he never complained, I knew that he missed the freedom of his previous life and the friends he had made along the way.

What set this chubby, sweet fellow apart from the other men was that he had never learned to speak like everyone else—he bellowed. He was just as loud whether you were standing in his face or a block away. Whenever he came home from a doctor's appointment, we could all hear him as he turned the corner of Washington Street, heading for Gift of Love, shouting happily to the world, "I'M HO-OME! I'M HO-OME!"

After Max died peacefully at Gift of Love, Sister Dominga and I were talking about the void we felt every time one of the men passed on. We both had to smile when she said that our friend Max was now probably approaching the gates of heaven crying out, "I'M HO-OME, I'M HO-OME!"

Afterword

In 2002, after twelve years of working with the dying, I was no longer able to continue. In 1996 I had been diagnosed with a progressive neurological disease, peripheral neuropathy, which I inherited from my mother. This disease was—and is—slowly destroying the nerves in my arms and legs, ultimately making it impossible for me to meet the physical demands of the work and the three flights of stairs at Gift of Love.

Since I am not inclined to sit home waiting for the neuropathy to take away my life, I have been greatly helped by physical therapy, which has kept my muscles functioning as best they can in spite of their increasing disconnection to the nerves. A cane often helps, and a friend's arm or shoulder keeps me on as steady a course as possible. I must add that the kindness of strangers when I travel around the big city of New York is inspiring.

When I had to stop my volunteer work for Mother Teresa, I realized that one thing I could still do was to share with others what I had learned during my years of working with the dying, including how I had dealt with the deaths of those I loved in my own family. The next step in my journey would be to write what I hoped would be of help to others.

For more than twenty years my spouse, Jim Russo, pursued a passion for collecting rare royal memorabilia and amassed quite an impressive collection, mostly from Russian Imperial families and British royalty. For me, the most fascinating part of Jim's collection was that each piece had historical significance. Among the many precious items in the collection were a Fabergé clock that was given by the Emperor of Russia, Alexander III, to his wife, the Empress Maria Fedorovna, on their twenty-fifth wedding anniversary, circa 1891, and a rare diamond and enamel bracelet given by the Emperor Alexander I to a family member in 1819.

After we toured Thailand and other third world countries in 2007, we both felt the need to start a foundation that would give disadvantaged children an opportunity to have an education and healthcare.

In order to raise money for this foundation, Jim decided that he would sell his beloved collection. For Jim, it was transforming one kind of love—the collection of beautiful historical things—into another kind of love: giving children a chance for a beautiful life.

Jim not only understands giving love to those in need around the world, but has also been blessed to be able to give comfort to his own loved ones.

Toward the end of his beloved sister Louise's life,

when she was in the last stages of cancer and bedridden most of the time, Jim half-carried Louise into the living room and gently eased her onto the sofa.

They were sitting quietly together, listening to music on the radio, when, for some inexplicable reason, Jim looked at his sister and asked, "Would you like to dance?"

Her face immediately lit up with a radiant glow, and she answered, "Yes!"

Knowing that it was no longer possible for her to actually dance, he lifted her up off the sofa and told her, "Just put your feet on mine."

And so they danced.

Louise had a faraway look in her eyes. When the song was over, Jim took her back to the sofa, where they sat together silently, holding hands, enveloped in the reverie of a memory that will last forever.

Whatever happens, we will try, in our own way, to follow Mother Teresa's simple words, "We can do no great things—only small things with great love."

I always say that Mother Teresa was an ordinary, extraordinary woman. Since my travels to the Far East I believe that, although she lived her life according to the teachings of the Catholic Church, she lived as much by the Buddhist philosophy as she did by the dogma of Catholicism. Mother Teresa believed in the simple words of the great teachers such as Jesus and Buddha and lived not a "Christian" life but a Christ*like* life—two very different things in my eyes. She tried to teach us all the simple philosophy of unconditional love for one another and the importance of being non-judgmental. Oh yes, and above all she wanted us to learn the joy of being of service with our two hands. Very simple and very beautiful.

Whatever may happen in the years to come, I will never forget the many wonderful men and women I helped in their final hours of life, and how much more they gave to me than I could ever have given to them. *Their* friendship and love will live with me forever, till we meet again in a far better place where we can all rejoice together. What a reunion that will be!

Praise for
Tony Cointreau's Award-Winning Memoir,
ETHEL MERMAN, MOTHER TERESA . . .
AND ME

It is magnificent. You made me laugh, and you made me cry. A lot. I don't know what I was expecting...it over-whelmed me, moved me in so many ways. When I was finished, I simply sat there . . .unable to talk...or to move . . . in the best way. You have written your own masterpiece . . . and I thank you for it.

— Barry Brown, Broadway Producer

. . . His descriptions of meeting and caring for people in Mother Teresa's facilities in the U.S. and Calcutta, India, are particularly moving . . . I have a love/hate relationship with memoirs. I'm sure most readers will lean toward the love part in Tony Cointreau's very moving and readable memoir.

— David M. Kinchen,
HuntingtonNews.net

I thoroughly enjoyed this book! And I highly recommend it to: anyone in a book club (great discussion opportunities within), anyone who is a fan of Ethel Merman or Mother Teresa, anyone who is poor wishing they were rich, anyone who wishes they were loved more as a child, to anyone who wants to serve and love others . . . to anyone: I recommend this book.

This memoir is beautifully written. It is captivating, heartbreaking, haunting, and inspiring.

— Margo Kelly, Blogger

For those of us who were not born into an uber wealthy old-money family, it's easy to think that all of our troubles would be over if only we had a whole lot of money. However, money does not necessarily mean that life is going to be easy. Tony Cointreau looked like someone who had it all, but life was empty and hard for him despite financial privilege. He dealt with dysfunction in his family and caretakers who caused him harm. As an adult, he set out to find meaning and purpose, and he succeeded. By learning to give himself to serve others, his life became meaningful. The memoir is inspiring and a great reminder that selfish pursuits are not what is truly important.

— Sweets4Bloggers

I found this memoir to be the most interesting I've read so far. It's well written. Mr. Cointreau is very candid in sharing his feelings and experiences, giving the reader the sense of personally knowing this extraordinary man. This memoir is definitely a page-turning, read-in-one-sitting, must-have for your book collection.

— Book Loons

Let me say right up front that this is a solicited review. I almost passed on the request. Over the last several years, I've set aside all but a couple of celebrity memoirs in a few chapters because the authors were so full of themselves... But something about the description of Tony Cointreau's book did ring true, and my fingers took on a life of their own as they typed out, "Yes, send it along." It was an inspired decision. I feel deeply moved and blessed by this book. The book reads like conversation with a friend... I also admired Cointreau's deft touch in setting an emotional tone. His heartwarming portraits of these remarkable women cut through the celebrity image to show them as human beings, ordinary in the sense of facing personal challenges most everyone can relate to... This beautiful story had me in tears increasingly often through the final section... Suffice it to say I felt ready to go forth and "do it unto the least of these..." when I closed the covers of this book.

— Sharon Lippincott, posted at GoodReads.com

Dear Tony,

I read your book this week. It's lovely. I finished it in a puddle of tears. What impresses me most is the easy, unaffected way that you tell your singular story. You made all the connections just perfectly. . . . Congratulations.

— Brian Kellow, author of
Ethel Merman, A Life

First, I want to say how beautiful this memoir is. You always hear the adage that money can't buy happiness and that message resounds loudly in this stunning memoir.... It's a story of hope, and unconditional love that is sure to keep you completely mesmerized. Cointreau writes as if he were sitting in your living room having a conversation with you. He is a spectacular story teller. I was enthralled with his interaction with Ethel Merman and Mother Teresa—such a gift. A beautiful memoir that covers many social issues as well as moral and emotional. A definite keeper and a must read!

— Wendy L. Hines, Vine Voice

With insight into a life of rare wealth and fortune, as well as horror and terror, Tony presents a marvelous memoir filled with endearing, courageous moments. Tony Cointreau allows us into his heart as we place him into ours.

— The Review Broads,
TheReviewBroads.com

To read this memoir is a rich, inspiring experience, with a little something for everyone within its memorable pages. Very nicely done!

— Crystal Book Reviews

… Your book left me both wrung out and inspired. Congratulations, dear Tony, both on the life you've lived, and the beautiful, sincere record you've made of it.

—Timothy Crouse, bestselling author of
Boys on the Bus

Featured story on Maria Shriver's website,
Powered by Inspiration: Igniting Architects of Change,
mariashriver.com — "How Mother Teresa and Ethel Merman Taught Me Unconditional Love,"
March 10, 2014.